CANTERBURY STUDIES IN SPIRITUAL THEOLOGY

Befc
King's Majesty

Lancelot Andrewes and His Writings

Edited by
Raymond Chapman

CANTERBURY
PRESS
Norwich

© in this compilation Raymond Chapman 2008

First published in 2008 by the Canterbury Press Norwich
(a publishing imprint of Hymns Ancient & Modern Limited,
a registered charity)
13–17 Long Lane, London EC1A 9PN

www.scm-canterburypress.co.uk

British Library Cataloguing in Publication data

A catalogue record for this book is available
from the British Library

ISBN 978-1-85311-889-0

Typeset by Regent Typesetting, London
Printed in the UK by
CPI William Clowes Beccles NR34 7TL

Contents

Editorial note		iv
Sources		vi
1	Introduction	1
2	Incarnation	18
3	Passion, Resurrection and Ascension	29
4	The Holy Spirit	44
5	Sacraments	52
6	Preaching	64
7	Scripture	71
8	Church and Ministry	78
9	Faith and Works	89
10	Law and Government	109
11	Devotional	125
Glossary		134
Further reading		136

Editorial Note

It is not easy to make a concise but representative selection from the work of Lancelot Andrewes. His sermons, like all good sermons, deserve to be worked through so that the development of doctrine and devotion can be fully savoured. What follows here is an attempt to show the main aspects of his thought and give some idea of his distinctive style. There is so much which still speaks to us today, that a little reading may encourage more exploration.

This selection concentrates mainly on his sermons, with some pieces from his catechistical work and a representation of his prayers. His polemical works, mainly directed against Roman claims, are not included. They are not edifying in this more ecumenical time, and as they are written in Latin they do not bring us close to the man's real voice.

The sermons are rich in quotations: biblical, patristic, sometimes classical, mostly in Latin, sometimes in Greek or Hebrew. Fortunately they are almost always followed immediately by the English rendering. For ease in continuous reading, I have omitted quotations in other languages, kept single quotation marks for direct quotations and made an English translation in the rare cases when he has not done so. Each sermon is headed by a note of the date and place of its preaching. The King James Version is used for the biblical texts on which they are based.

By the early seventeenth century, written English was settling into an accepted convention which would not radically change and is not opaque today. Some words have become obsolete or changed their meaning, and a glossary of these is provided. Biblical names are not glossed unless they appear in an unfamiliar form. It can fairly be assumed that readers having some acquaintance with Shakespeare, the Book of Common Prayer and the King James Version of the Bible will have no difficulty with forms like 'saith' and 'teacheth' or the singular second person pronouns. Capital letters have been kept as Andrewes used them for divine pronouns and some nouns, as has his occasional use of italics. The aim has been to make his work accessible to the modern reader without unnecessary impediments but without losing the distinctive flavour of his time and his own style.

The word 'Anglican' is used to avoid continual repetition of 'Belonging or pertaining to the Church of England', although it does not seem to have been current in the lifetime of Andrewes. 'Puritan' similarly avoids attempts to differentiate the various aspects and degrees of opposition to the Established Church. As this is not a detailed exercise in ecclesiastical history, one name must cover those who were dissatisfied with the extent and direction of changes following the Reformation, disliked episcopacy in the form it had taken, and found the Book of Common Prayer not sufficiently reformed. It includes those who wanted changes within the Church, and those who set up separate religious organizations. It is not intended to indicate simply a tall hat and a gloomy expression.

[ ] denotes editorial additions or comments within extracts.

[. . .] denotes editorial omissions from the original text.

< > denotes expansion of initials or abbreviations in the text.

Sources

Ninety-six Sermons, 5 vols, Oxford: Parker, 1851–3; referenced by season or occasion with volume number and pages, e.g. Nativity sermon 8, vol. 1, pp. 118–20

Opuscula Quaedam Posthuma, Oxford: Parker, 1852

A Pattern of Catechistical Doctrine and other Minor Works, Oxford: Parker, 1846

The Preces Privatae of Lancelot Andrewes, Bishop of Winchester, trans. F. E. Brightman, London: Methuen, 1903

Two Answers to Cardinal Perron and Other Miscellaneous Works, Oxford: Parker, 1854

The sermons were issued as a folio volume by William Laud and John Buckeridge, Bishop of Rochester, in 1629, arranged by their places in the liturgical year. They were reprinted in the same form as part of the *Library of Anglo-Catholic Theology*, 1851–3, which remains the only complete edition and is used in the present book. Some selections have been published more recently, arranged by the place or time of their delivery. Readers who seek a fuller discussion of texts and sources are referred to the Introduction to P. McCullough (ed.), *Lancelot Andrewes: Selected Sermons and Lectures*, Oxford: OUP, 2005.

I

Introduction

Life

There has never been a Golden Age except in legends and the imagination of poets. The Tractarian vision of the Stuart Church as an ideal to which a degenerate age should seek to return needs to be modified by the reality of much conflict and intrigue, despite the undoubted quality of many of its divines and writers. Lancelot Andrewes was a great influence for good in that troubled time, and in the years that followed. Most of his work was done in the reign of the first Stuart monarch, but it needs to be remembered that he was essentially an Elizabethan. He was born in 1554, ten years before Shakespeare, and he grew up in the period of extremes and paradoxes, of confidence and anxiety, magnificence and squalor, nobility and cruelty, which those plays reveal. He was thirty-four at the time of the Spanish Armada, a victory which took on an iconic significance for the next generation. By the time he came to be a power in the Church of England, it had gained a new assurance, but was still torn by attacks from without and disputes within. It needed the deep piety, the learning and the desire for peace of men like Andrewes.

By his own testimony, he was born in the parish of All Hallows, Barking, one of the eastern suburbs into which London was beginning to thrust its growing population. He was the first of thirteen children of Thomas Andrewes, a Suffolk man who had been a mariner and became a Master of Trinity House. Young Lancelot began his education at the Cooper's Free School, Radcliffe, before moving to the Merchant Taylors', a school which had won a high reputation under the formidable and learned Richard Mulcaster, noted among other things for his praise of the English language even above the Latin which was the foundation of the Elizabethan curriculum. Andrewes, already showing his love of learning, became head scholar before going in 1571 as a scholar to Pembroke Hall, Cambridge. In the same year he was named as a scholar of Jesus College, Oxford. He took his Oxford MA in 1581 but there is no record of his residence, which, in view of the lack of funds in this the newly founded college, suggests that his membership was only titular.

Cambridge at this time was noted for its evangelical tendencies, dating back to the days when Cranmer and others were debating Lutheran ideas there. Pembroke had a particularly strong Puritan representation, active in prayer meetings and 'prophesyings'. Andrewes would later have much to say against Puritans but as an undergraduate his main interest was in his studies. In his later life he studied all the morning and again in the evening. As a leading churchman, close to the affairs of State, he was never so active in the public sphere as in writing and preaching. At the beginning of the university vacations he walked to London. It is said that he studied a new subject each time he was at home. He was reputed to have mastered fifteen languages, ancient and modern. He graduated as BA in 1575, becoming a Fellow of Pembroke, MA in 1578 and BD in 1585. During his time at Pembroke he held the office of Catechist and produced his first printed work, *A Pattern of Catechistical Doctrine*. The importance of systematic instruction was emphasized in all the churches of the time; Andrewes opened the way for later Anglican catechistical writers like Nicholson, Hammond, Sherlock, and Ken.

Despite his devotion to scholarship, he was being drawn into public affairs at a time of tension and uncertainty. Plots against the Queen added to fears of the Spanish threat, which culminated in the defeat of the Armada in 1588. In 1586 Andrewes accompanied the Earl of Huntingdon, President of the Council of the North, as his chaplain, and apparently disputed with and convinced some Romanists in northern counties. He was subsequently a chaplain to the Queen and to Whitgift, Archbishop of Canterbury. He gained the approval and patronage of Francis Walsingham, Elizabeth's Secretary of State and head of her efficient intelligence service, and preferment began to come his way. In 1589 he became Vicar of St Giles, Cripplegate, and received prebends at both St Paul's Cathedral and Southwell. In the same year he was elected Master of Pembroke. Such Church pluralities seem today to be scandalous and unjustifiable, but they were accepted as the lot of clergy who had influential support, then and for long afterwards. He did not treat them as mere sinecures: when he held the post of Penitentiary at St Paul's, he would walk in the cathedral ready to hear confessions and give counsel. It was not an office widely used or approved, and a sermon on absolution preached in 1600 (p. 81) aroused controversy.

His reputation as an apologist for the Church of England was growing. He was sent to confer with John Udal, imprisoned on suspicion of being involved with the Marprelate tracts, and the Separatist Henry Barrow. He argued against the Lambeth Articles issued in 1595 by a group of Puritan sympathizers who met with Archbishop Whitgift. The Articles were given no authority, and the Queen disapproved of them, but the minor controversy was significant in marking Andrewes as an opponent of the extreme Calvinist position. In 1600 he became Dean of Westminster. He did not give up his other posts, but again he did not treat his new position lightly. He took a great interest in Westminster School, taught some of the senior boys and took them on walks, and gained a reputation as a kind and patient teacher which was far from general among Elizabethan schoolmasters.

Elizabeth I died in 1603. After years of intrigue and anxiety, James VI of Scotland came peacefully south as James I of England. He arrived in London during a severe outbreak of the plague, in which as many as ten per cent of the population may have died. Andrewes took refuge for a time in Chiswick, to the west of London, but he was present at the coronation in Westminster Abbey of the King before whom he would give most of the sermons on which his reputation chiefly rests.

On his way south, James had been met by a number of Presbyterian divines, who presented him with a series of demands for changes in Church usage. In response to the Millenary Petition, as it was called, James convened a conference at Hampton Court in 1604. The petitioners won few concessions, but the request for a new translation of the Bible was approved and a committee of forty-seven, including some on the Puritan side, was set up to begin the work. It was to be taken from the Hebrew and Greek originals, though in practice the existing Great Bible was closely followed. There were to be none of the marginal notes that had made the Geneva Bible contentious, except glosses on Hebrew and Greek words. Andrewes was made chairman of the 'company', one of six, to be responsible for the books from Genesis to 2 Kings. The result was the Authorized, or King James, Version, published in 1611, which with the Book of Common Prayer supported public and private devotion across the centuries.

In 1605 Andrewes became Bishop of Chichester. It was not a rich diocese, but he now resigned his posts at Westminster, St Giles and Pembroke. He had refused previous offers of sees because of his objection to alienation of resources, against which he had earlier protested in his doctoral dissertation *Sacrilege a Snare*. In 1609 he was translated to Ely and in 1618 to Winchester, a diocese with a strong Puritan presence. His Visitation Articles were firm and searching, determined to maintain order and decency in parish worship. They express more legalistically what he said in preaching against inattention to the sermon:

> We come to it if we will, we go our ways when we will, stay no longer than we will, and listen to it while we will; and sleep out, or turn us and talk out or sit still and let our minds rove the rest whither they will; take stitch at a phrase or word, and censure it how we will. So the word serves us to make us sport; we serve not it.
>
> Gunpowder Treason sermon 9

He attended to the buildings under his charge and caused repairs to be made at Westminster, Chichester, and Ely, and the Bishop of Winchester's London palace, Southwark.

Although Winchester was a large and important diocese, Andrewes might well have expected higher preferment when Canterbury became vacant in 1610. The man appointed was George Abbot, who had assisted James in trying to impose a more Anglican pattern on the Church in Scotland. He was also more amenable than Andrewes to royal intervention in Church affairs, and more inclined to the Calvinism that the King favoured. Abbot was not a great success as Archbishop and later became involved in trouble from which Andrewes helped to save him. In 1621 Abbot accidentally shot and killed a keeper while out hunting. Although there was no criminal intent, this act of homicide exposed him to both civil and ecclesiastical penalties. The King remitted his legal obligation and Andrewes supported his freedom from ecclesiastical suspension.

Andrewes had been concerned with more things than the care of his dioceses, and it is necessary to go back to 1605. The Gunpowder Plot to blow up the King and Parliament together was revealed on 3 November. Two days later, Andrewes, just appointed to Chichester, would have been in the Lords and died with the rest if the plot had succeeded. The date was appointed to be kept as a day of public thanksgiving. Andrewes delivered the 'Gunpowder Treason' sermon before the King for many years, with a fervour that is understandable in view of his narrow escape, together with anger at the sacrilege of the plot being claimed by the conspirators as a religious act.

Most English Roman Catholics were loyal to the Crown, but the Plot led to a surge of Anti-Roman feeling and bitter controversy. Andrewes entered into a debate conducted in Latin with the prominent papal apologist Cardinal Bellarmine, who had attacked the Oath of Allegiance issued by James after the Gunpowder Plot, which denied the right of the

Pope to absolve subjects from their allegiance to the civil ruler. Andrewes responded with a defence in Latin, *Tortura Torti*, refuting the papal claim to supremacy over the Church, and the power to dispense subjects from their civil loyalty. When Bellarmine made a further attack, Andrewes replied with a *Responsio*. By the second decade of the seventeenth century, the Anglican voice was becoming more confident. The Church of England would not accept either the Roman claim or the extreme Puritan idea of an 'invisible' Church without formal hierarchical structure, but asserted itself as fully Catholic, in true succession to the early undivided Church. Andrewes made the profession that would be repeated by generations of Anglican apologists:

> One canon reduced to writing by God himself, two testaments, three creeds, four general councils, five centuries, and the series of Fathers in that period – the centuries, that is, before Constantine, and two after – determine the boundary of our faith.

> *Opuscula*, p. 91

Contacts with the Reformed Churches on the Continent were generally less acrimonious, but not always smooth. In 1610 Archbishop Bancroft invited the Swiss scholar Isaac Casaubon to England. He met Andrewes, read and commented on his *Responsio*, and came to accept the Anglican claim to be a true part of the Catholic Church. The King rewarded him with a pension and a prebend in Canterbury Cathedral. Relations were less cordial with Hugo Grotius, a leading Dutch jurist and theologian, who came to England in 1613 but did not persuade James to accept his Arminian view. Writing a few years later, Andrewes said that Grotius gave too much power to civil authority over the Church. Matters of faith were to be decided by synods of bishops and others, not by the King or lay authorities. Further, priests had authority to loose or retain sins; excommunication was a real ecclesiastical jurisdiction; episcopacy was essential to a true Church. This last point was one of the major ecclesiastical issues of the time. Andrewes and those who thought like him believed episcopacy to be divinely ordained. There were those who held that it was for the 'godly prince' to decide whether a national Church should have bishops, an order which might be good for the Church but not of its essence; Churches without bishops were not necessarily invalid. Others said that there was no difference of orders in ministry, only degrees of jurisdiction. Andrewes was not one of the English representatives at the Synod of Dort which met in 1618 to debate issues between Calvinists and Arminians, and ended in a victory for the extreme Calvinist position. The Arminians denied certain strict Calvinist tenets, mainly on three points: that Christ died only for the elect, that grace was irresistible, and that the elect were incapable of falling from grace.

Andrewes became Court Preacher in 1605. He had already often preached before the monarch, but now he preached at Christmas, Easter and Whitsun, and the anniversary of the Gunpowder Plot, for the next nineteen years. He also gave the Gowrie Conspiracy sermon annually on 5 August. This was an anniversary fervently recalled by James I, although not comparable in public importance to the Gunpowder Plot. On that day in 1600 James, still King only of Scotland, was persuaded to go to the house of the Earl of Gowrie in Perth, where an attempt was made on his life by the earl's brother. The King escaped unhurt and both the brothers were killed. The story was confused and not wholly consistent, and was not universally believed. Nevertheless, a special service was ordered, and maintained for many years, though it never gained the position of a State Service in the Prayer Book.

As Court Preacher, Andrewes became close to the King and his entourage. It was not an attractive milieu for a devout scholar; it was disorderly, permeated with favouritism and intrigue, though probably no worse than most royal courts at that time. James I was nervous, sometimes uncouth in manner, generally coarse and untidy in his person. He was also a good scholar, a collector of pictures and other objects of art, and keenly interested in theology. His personal belief tended to Calvinism, not to the Arminian position that was strong, though not universal, among senior English churchmen, and would become dominant in the next reign under Charles I and William Laud. Despite all these unpromising factors, James had great respect for Andrewes; some said that he was the only man of whom the King stood in awe.

For his part, Andrewes took a very high view of monarchy, although as his reply to Grotius showed, he would not yield any ground in regard to Church rights and strictly ecclesiastical matters. In all else, he defended the divine rights of the anointed monarch, a position continuing the medieval view and strengthened by the rejection of a rival power in the papacy. As his thought on the matter evolved, it became stronger; monarchs had duties as well as rights, but even bad monarchs were to be honoured and obeyed.

Although he was close to the King, in a period when leading churchmen were often drawn into affairs of state, he seems to have had little direct influence over political matters. As Lord Almoner he had the task of dispensing royal alms, and discretion over surplus; he resigned from this post on becoming Dean of the Chapels Royal in 1618. He was a member of the Court of High Commission, and sat on many committees of the House of Lords for both ecclesiastical and secular matters. In 1616 he was brought on to the Privy Council, any member of which could sit in the Court of Star Chamber. It was here that he took part in the trial for heresy of John Traske; an extract from his judgement is given on page 74.

His only major role in public affairs was one which has received much, and perhaps excessive, attention from his biographers. In 1601 Robert Devereux, Earl of Essex, son of the disgraced and executed favourite of Elizabeth I, married Frances Howard, the daughter of the Earl of Suffolk. He was fourteen and she thirteen; such early marriages among the aristocracy were not uncommon at the time. After some years Frances became infatuated with Robert Carr, Viscount Rochester, a close favourite of James, and sought to end the marriage. In 1613 Essex agreed to allow her to bring a suit for nullity but would not admit impotence except towards his wife. It was alleged that she had taken measures, including witchcraft, to prevent consummation. Andrewes was appointed to the divorce commission. The case was bitterly disputed, with publicity as lurid as that which attended some nineteenth-century divorce scandals. The King wanted a decision in favour of divorce and demanded a plain verdict for or against. At this, Abbot and several other members of the commission who opposed the plea withdrew. Andrewes seems to have been against the divorce, but to have changed his stance after James I urged him to support it. Whether it was from his habitual respect for the royal word, a timid desire to please, or a genuine change of mind, his agreement has been regarded as a blot on his reputation for integrity and holiness. All that need now be said is that the affair is long since gone, that no one goes through life without imperfection, and that it is only a basically good man who could arouse so much opposition for a single lapse.

After James I died in 1625, Andrewes did not preach again in the presence of the King. He was over seventy, and in failing health, and the Church of England was soon to take a new turn under William Laud. Charles I respected his father's royal preacher, later arranged for his sermons to be printed, and commended them to the Princess Elizabeth on the eve of his execution. Andrewes's last public act was to take a small part in the coronation. He died peacefully on 25 May 1626 after a slow decline during which he spent most of his time in prayer. His funeral went from Winchester House, the episcopal palace that he had helped to repair, to his interment in St Saviour's, Southwark. His tomb was moved in 1830 to the west end of the Lady Chapel in what is now Southwark Cathedral. There his effigy lies, vested in chimere and rochet, with the mantle of the Garter. A more appropriate memorial than these honours of Church and State is the book in his right hand.

He was admired by his contemporaries and by those who came immediately after him. Many recorded his piety, the constancy and intensity of his personal prayers, and the austerity of his life. He was remembered as charitable and benevolent, both in money and in giving ecclesiastical preferment to 'divers eminent men in learning' who had no special claim on him. His first biographer Henry Isaacson, who had lived in his house as his amanuensis, testified that 'He was ever hospitable, and free in entertainment to all people of quality and worthy of respect, especially to scholars and strangers'. His learning was prodigious, even for a time when, unlike today, leading divines had ample time for reading if they so chose. Isaacson believed that 'If he had been contemporary with the ancient fathers of the primitive Church, he would have been, and that worthily, reputed not inferior to the chiefest among them'. Andrewes, who attached so much value to the patristic writers, would have been content with that tribute.

Teaching

The genius of Andrewes was to combine learning and devotion in powerful teaching of the faith and its practical implications. He was not a systematic theologian like Calvin, or his Anglican contemporary Hooker; in fact he distrusted theological systems and had little time for the precise definitions which both Puritans and Romanists were prepared to use in their controversy with the emerging Church of England. He was totally devoted to that Church, in the conviction that it was a continuing part of the Catholic Church, purified of errors but resistant to new doctrines and structures. He believed that every Church that had kept the continuity of faithful tradition was in communion with all who held the faith given by Christ to the Apostles. The Church of England had authority so long as it remained true to apostolic faith and practice. For him, the Church was not an ideal abstract concept but, in the words of the Prayer Book, 'the blessed company of all faithful people'. The fervour of his preaching was largely directed towards reminding his hearers of the grace they had received and their responsibilities as members of the Body of Christ.

Though he did not emulate Jewel and Hooker, who from their different approaches had attempted a structured defence of their Church, he was a great Anglican apologist who was influential in his own time and beyond. He addressed the question that his contemporaries were discussing, and which would continue to preoccupy Anglican thinkers for centuries to come. Their aim was to present the Church of England as a *via media* which was not just a negative rejection of the Roman and extreme Reformed positions, but a true expression of what had been handed down from the beginning. It was essential to prove the historical basis for her doctrine, order and governance. To this end, Andrewes searched Scripture and studied the patristic writings to support his case.

At the same time, he had a wider vision, a desire for Christian unity and reconciliation that was not common at that time. He hoped for an end to controversy in the universal Church. He shared with Hooker a sense of the wholeness of the Church and its traditions, a desire to be part of the continuity of Christians who held to the historic creeds and kept the apostolic tradition. A strong defender of episcopacy, he was willing to concede recognition to Churches that for sufficient reason were without bishops in the apostolic succession. But his abiding power lies in his promulgating his belief in the tones of quiet Anglican devotion.

His theology was mystical rather than speculative, refusing to make a system of a mystery. Like many of the Early Fathers whom he so much admired, his belief led him not to thinking intellectually about God but to trying to express the experience granted by God through revelation. This is not to say that his teaching was vague, or comprehensive rather than detailed. There were aspects of faith that particularly concerned him. Some of his most powerful sermons are on the Incarnation, which established a new relationship between man and God. He tells how the Passion brings liberation from the captivity of sin, the Resurrection destroys death, the Ascension raises humanity to the right hand of the Father, Pentecost enables humanity to respond to God's call and share in the divine life. These basic tenets of the Christian faith are presented by him with urgency, imagination and a continual sense of rediscovery for each day and each believer.

From the richness of his thought, examples of some of these themes have been selected, presented in the following order.

The Nativity sermons contain much of his most eloquent preaching. He held a strong incarnational doctrine, never ceasing to marvel at the union of the divine and human natures. He urged his hearers to accept the true humanity of Christ, to beware of any Docetic suggestion that his manhood was a mere appearance. He continually returned to the humility of the human birth, the acceptance of limitation, the marvel of hidden divinity.

Andrewes did not make the mystery of the Incarnation a remote wonder, a single event in history. He put forward the idea that was found among the Greek Fathers of *theosis*, the taking of our human nature into the godhead. In the words of Athanasius, 'He became man that we might become God'. It is a great theme, perhaps easily misunderstood and taken too literally, but Andrewes presented it well. Our knowledge of God can become perfect through love and a devout sense of identification with the humanity of our Lord. It is significant that so many of his Nativity sermons end with invitation to the Eucharist and promise of the heavenly banquet where human souls are brought into the eternal presence of God.

No preacher can fail to try to expound something of the mystery that is commemorated in the events from Good Friday to the Feast of the Ascension. Andrewes spoke with deep feeling about the Passion, relating it to the Old Testament prophecies, urging his hearers to remember that it was not the Jewish people alone but the whole human race that shared the guilt of the Crucifixion. But it is what follows that most inspired him; the Easter joy is present proleptically in the Passion, the day that we rightly name 'Good Friday'.

He preached eighteen sermons on the Resurrection, on every Easter Day from 1606 to 1624. In the greatest Christian festival the Nativity themes were fulfilled. Christmas celebrates a wonderful birth, Easter a new birth even more wonderful. Christmas tells of divinity emptying itself and accepting human limitation, Easter the fully human again assuming full divinity. The world is given a new hope, a changed attitude to death. The vision of *theosis* is fulfilled in the perpetual union of the Risen Christ and humanity.

Pneumatology, doctrine concerning the Holy Spirit, is not a prominent feature of the theology in his time. Andrewes was notable for his Whitsun preaching, here again influenced by patristic thought. He saw the need to declare the importance of the Holy Spirit, in danger of being diminished by the concentration of many contemporary preachers on Christ alone, to the detriment of Trinitarian doctrine. At the same time, he needed to counter the excesses of some extremists who claimed special power from the Holy Spirit to justify and exalt their private judgement. His position was that the work of Christ and of the Holy Spirit are inseparable, leading the believer towards *theosis*. Belief in the Holy Spirit is an essential part of the economy of salvation, authenticating the redemptive action of Christ: this is one of the distinctive points in the doctrine that he preached.

He links the work of the Holy Spirit in the world to the unceasing activities of the Church, especially in baptism and the Eucharist, but also through preaching. Listening to sermons is important but it is not enough unless it leads to informed prayer. A great preacher himself, he was against excessive and disordered preaching – essentially a sacramentalist. Not everyone receives the gift of preaching, and the preacher must be properly called and authorized by the Church.

The Holy Spirit is powerful in the ordination of priests and the consecration of bishops; with the words 'Receive the Holy Ghost', the fullness of grace is given. But this grace is offered freely to all who will accept it, and contrary to strict Calvinist teaching, he holds that it is possible to resist and reject it. There is a special grace of ordained ministry but every Christian has a vocation though not all at the same level. Against the Puritans, he maintained that bishop and priest are distinct orders. He asserted the validity of Anglican orders as being in the apostolic succession, with power to celebrate the sacraments, and to absolve from repented sins. Accepting the catholic doctrine stated in the words of the Twenty-sixth Article of Religion, 'Of the unworthiness of the Ministers, which hinders not the effect of the Sacrament', he yet demanded a high standard of life for the clergy, and for the sound learning which so many lacked – not a surprising deficiency in that age of pluralities and ill-paid benefices.

The Eucharist is the supreme means through which the Christian obtains the grace of the Holy Spirit. It is in this sacrament that the Church continues to live out the whole work of salvation in the world. Andrewes held a high doctrine of the Eucharist, rejecting both the subtle definition of transubstantiation and the receptionism of some of the Reformers. His eucharistic theology may be seen as typically Anglican, close to that of Hooker. We need to know the reality of union with the Body of Christ but not to seek intellectual understanding of the mystery. His belief in the Real Presence is linked to his assurance of the reality of the Incarnation. There is a kind of hypostatic union between Christ and the eucharistic elements, as there is between his divine and human natures.

While he did not adhere to the Reformed doctrine of *sola scriptura*, Scripture alone, his sacramentalism did not make him undervalue the authority of the Bible. His preaching is rooted in it, continually upheld and proved by it. He would draw on both Testaments, finding analogies for the New in the Old, proclaiming the Word of God as revealed in the written word. As his indictment of Traske shows, he was not patient with those who would appeal to the Jewish Law and usage to justify deviation from orthodox Christian practice. Nor did he approve of private interpretations of the Bible as uttered by unlicensed preachers and Puritan 'prophesyings'. The Church is the allowed interpreter, and he defended Anglican readings against Roman claims to sole authority in the matter.

Strong for faith in the doctrine of the Bible and the tradition of the Church, throughout his preaching he also commanded the response of obedience through the individual life. The comparative role of faith and works has never been an 'either-or' choice in orthodox theology, but it has continued to nag at Christian thinkers from the New Testament to Luther, and beyond. The doctrinal arguments which had fuelled the Reformation and Counter-Reformation were by now leading to fresh considerations of moral theology, no longer content with the medieval Scholastic systems but looking afresh at the Bible and the early Fathers. Andrewes had no doubt that right belief and right living must always go together; in more recent terms, orthodoxy needs to be fulfilled in orthopraxis.

He certainly had no inclination to the Pelagian, teaching that the human will could itself work towards salvation. Nor did he go as far as the Lutheran Philip Melancthon in suggesting that the human will works effectively in the process of conversion. Yet this idea of 'synergy' was not entirely uncongenial to him; salvation is the free gift of God alone, but the will of the believer must collaborate with the grace given through the Holy Spirit to attain the longed-for *theosis*. The image of God remains even in our fallen state, marred but not erased. Good works are needed as well as good dispositions. He preached the duty of perseverance, not with the Calvinist certainty that grace could not be resisted or elected salvation lost, but as a continual demonstration of faith and as gratitude for the salvation which works alone could not earn. This is well illustrated in his sermon on the journey of the Magi (p. 26) in which he gives a long exposition of the need not only for 'seeing' but also for 'coming'. The discipline of the Church was to be obeyed in matters like fasting, seeking absolution after repentance, and the custom of 'ashing' on Ash Wednesday.

His high regard for monarchy has already been discussed. As for any Anglican of the time, or anyone in the Lutheran tradition, ecclesiastical and secular authority were not opposed but symbiotic. As his early biographer Isaacson wrote, he wanted always 'to raise a joint reverence to God and the Prince, to the spiritual and civil Magistrate, by uniting and not severing them'. Some of his ideas are hard to comprehend today and were strong even for his time, but they are inextricably part of his thought. The anointed sovereign participates in the royalty of Christ and is above ordinary humanity, the leader towards *theosis*, by virtue of his royal priesthood in the priesthood of all believers. Since the sovereign holds power ordained by God, there can be no question of a just revolt. None but God can make or remove a Christian ruler: papal claims to a right of deposition were utterly false.

These things he taught, especially in the Gunpowder and Gowrie sermons but not in them alone. Sometimes his words may read today as severe and uncharitable, when he seems to delight in the destruction of public enemies. For all its elegance and piety, it was a hard and often cruel age; and a man who had narrowly escaped being blown to pieces had some reason not to forget past conspiracies, and to believe that deliverance from enemies was an act of God. Nor did he believe that the sovereign was exempt from the duties of the ordinary Christian. The one who rules has duties to the Church and to the people, and must hold office with humility and dependence on God.

Finally, he has been remembered most frequently for his published prayers. The *Preces Privatae*, 'Private Prayers', have gone through a number of translations and editions. They are largely an assembly of quotations, from the Bible, from western and eastern liturgies, from Synagogue worship. Yet he worked on them in such a way that the result seems fresh and whole, an epitome of the quiet devotion, with a strong penitential emphasis, which may be seen as a distinctive feature of the Anglican ethos. Morning and Evening prayer are provided for every day of the week, and there are prayers for the traditional aspects of thanksgiving, penitence, petition and intercession. The subjects for intercession reveal the breadth of his awareness and sympathy. Within a long sequence of prayers for various needs and causes, he remembers to pray for:

Yeomen, merchantmen, handicraftsmen, even down to sordid crafts and the beggars: for the rising generation whether in universities or in schools, that, as in age, so they may increase in wisdom withal, and in favour with God and man.

Preces Privatae, p. 270

These prayers were intended mainly for his own use, and that gives them a sense of immediacy and personal experience that in turn makes them personal for private devotions today. He has been there, brought his

concerns into the presence of God, and left a way open for future generations. These are prayers that never seem to be coldly intellectual; they
draw the whole person into colloquy with God. Some extracts are here
printed, with other examples of his thoughts on prayer.

Style

Andrewes took the responsibility of preaching very seriously. He was
intolerant of those who came late to the service and fulfilled the obligation of attendance by being just in time to hear the sermon, or who
listened passively and did not take the message into their lives. It was not
something to be undertaken lightly or routinely: when he was at St
Giles' Cripplegate, he said that 'When he preached twice a day he prated
once'. There were many testimonies to his eloquence and compelling
manner in the pulpit, and his power of reaching to the hearts of his
hearers.

. The sermons as they have come down to us are headed with his text,
in Latin and in an English translation that is sometimes from one of the
versions available in his day and sometimes probably his own rendering.
They naturally vary in structure according to the occasion and his inten-
tion, but they tend to follow a similar development. He expounds the
message or act of God that is found in the text, explains its relevance to
the present age, and declares the response that should follow in the lives
of those who have heard it, usually ending with a prayer or an ascription
of adoration. His method is exegetical, drawing out the meaning of text
and context, supporting his interpretation by copious references to
other biblical passages and to patristic writings. Like other leading
Anglican divines of the time, he looked to the early Fathers rather than
the medieval scholastics. His purpose was not to get his congregation
thinking intellectually and analytically about God but to convey to them
through language the experience of life lived in God. Thought and
reason are not set aside, but their use is to contribute towards a deeper
insight into faith.

To this end, the familiar words of faith are examined in various mean-
ings applied to the text. An example is the second Lent sermon, where
his text 'By the hand of Moses and Aaron' leads him to a succession of
images from the anatomical details of the human hand to the idea of
God's directing providence (pp. 94ff.). He draws on the Old Testament
typology much valued by the Fathers. The twelfth Resurrection sermon

begins with a close exegesis of Christ's own words comparing the three days in the Tomb to the days of Jonah in the great fish. The biblical use of allegory and personification is a gift to him. In the eleventh Nativity sermon he has a fine time with the Psalmist's meeting of Mercy and Truth, Righteousness and Peace (pp. 104ff.). He can see delivery from the Gunpowder Plot as replicating the Old Testament mercies of Passover and Purim (p. 120).

He engages with the paradoxes in Christianity, the seeming contradictions which express realities beyond ordinary comprehension. He knew that orthodox faith must continually accept the 'both-and' of revealed truth, and that 'either-or' is the road to heresy. He delights in the thought of the Infant Christ, *infans* meaning 'without speech', who is the incarnate Word – 'The word without a word; the eternal Word not able to speak a word' (p. 23). He affirms succinctly the supreme paradox of the Incarnation:

> God before eternally, and now today Man; and so both, and takes hold of both, and brings both together again. For two natures here are in Him. If conceived and born of a woman, then a man; if God with us, then God.
>
> Nativity sermon 9

The reader of his sermons is in no doubt that they are directed to a listening assembly. Their manner is colloquial, different in style from his formal writings. Failing to make spiritual advance is not to be static but to regress, 'as they that row against the stream, if they hold still, are carried backward' (p. 91). Connection with heresy makes 'a piece of linsey-woolsey of Christian religion' (p. 74). The bishop could remember the small boy in a London street, watching a skilled butcher at work:

> Dividing implies skill to hit the joint right; for that is to divide. To cut at venture, quite beside the joint, it skills not where, through skin and bones and all; that is to chop and mangle, and not to divide.
>
> p. 103

It was the son of a mariner who said:

> They talk of discoveries, and much ado is made of a new passage found out to this or that place: what say you to this discovery 'on high', this passage into the 'land of the living'? Sure it passes all. And

this discovery is here, and upon this discovery there is begun a commerce, or trade of intercourse, between Heaven and us.

p. 43

He uses pithy, startling phrases that seem to bring us close to the sound
of Jacobean speech. He thinks how people of his own time would not
hasten with the Magi to see the newborn Christ. 'Christ is no wildcat.
What talk ye of twelve days? And if it be forty days hence, ye shall be
sure to find His Mother and Him; she cannot be churched till then.
What needs such haste?' (p. 28).

He also makes full use of the devices and figures of rhetoric that were
taught in the educational system of the time and would engage the interest of his auditors. He plays on words and their sounds: 'He that cometh
here in clouts, He will come in the clouds one day.' He delights in the
classical figures of speech – see his overt use of synecdoche (p. 104). Yet
these things never give the impression of being used for effect alone. They
are linguistic means to a devotional end, and they make their point.
Often the complex structure of a rhetorical figure is followed by a
sequence of short sentences, even one lacking a main verb, which drives
home as if with a blow on the pulpit the point that he has been making.
'A gardener He is then. The first, the fairest garden that ever was,
Paradise, He was the gardener, it was of His planting. So, a gardener'
(p. 36).

He has been regarded as one of the pioneers of the Metaphysical style
of preaching with its conceits, puns, analogies, and antitheses. Sometimes indeed he will torment an idea and stretch a word as ingeniously
as John Donne; thus taking 'Immanuel', 'God with us':

If without Him in this <world>, without Him in the next; and if without Him there – if it be not *Immanu-el*, it will be *Immanu-hell*; [. . .]
What with Him? Why, if we have Him, and God by Him, we need no
more; *Immanu-el* and *Immanu-all*.

Nativity sermon 9

The style fell from favour later in the seventeenth century. In 1683 John
Evelyn noted in his diary having heard a preacher who 'preached much
after Bish<op> Andrewes's method, full of logical divisions, in short and
broken periods, and Latin sentences [. . .] now quite out of fashion in the
pulpit'. Long afterwards, T.S. Eliot found that the sermons were still
vigorous and memorable:

When Andrewes begins his sermon, from beginning to end you are sure that he is wholly in his subject, unaware of anything else, that his emotion grows as he penetrates more deeply into his subject, that he is finally 'alone with the Alone', with the mystery which he is trying to grasp more and more firmly.

T. S. Eliot, *For Lancelot Andrewes: Essays on Style and Order*, London: Faber 1928, p. 29

2

Incarnation

Before James I at Whitehall, Christmas Day 1609

God sent forth His Son, made of a woman, made under the law.

Galatians 4.4–5

The deep reality of the Incarnation: the Son became truly and fully human and accepted the condition of fallen humanity. Our rejoicing in the Nativity should honour it through the Eucharist.

But 'made' man. First I will ask with David; 'Lord, what is man?' And then tell you his answer, 'Man is like a thing of nought'. And this He was 'made', this He became 'made' man, 'made of a woman'; 'did not abhor the virgin's womb', as we sing daily to the high praise of the fullness of His humility, to which His love brought Him for our sakes. For whatsoever else He had been 'made', it would have done us no good. In this then was 'the fullness' of His love, as before of His Father's – that He would be made, and was made, not what was fittest for Him, but what was best for us; not what was most for His glory, but what was most for our benefit and behoof.

'Made of a woman'. For man He might have been 'made', and yet have had a body framed for Him in Heaven; and not 'made of a woman'. But when He saith, 'Made of a woman', it is evident that He passed not through her as water through a conduit pipe, as fondly dreameth the Anabaptist. 'Made of': Made of her; she ministered the matter, 'flesh of her flesh', 'the seed'; and the principal and very inward chief part of the substance. Made of that, made of her very substance.

And so have we here now in one both twain His natures; 'God sent His Son' – there His divine; 'made of a woman' – here His human nature. That, from the bosom of His Father before all worlds; this from the womb of His mother in the world. So that as from eternity God His

Father might say that verse of the Psalm, 'Thou art My Son, this day have I begotten Thee'. So in 'the fullness of time' might the Virgin His mother no less truly, 'Thou art my Son this day have I brought Thee into the World'.

And here now at this word; 'made of a woman', He beginneth to concern us somewhat. There groweth an alliance between us; for we also are made of a woman. And our hope is as He will not be confounded to be counted 'among those born of woman' no more will He be, saith the Apostle, 'to acknowledge us His brethren'. And so by this time He groweth somewhat near us.

This now is full for the union with our nature, to be 'made of a woman'. But so to be 'made of a woman' without He be also 'made under the Law', is not near enough yet. For if He be out of the compass of the law that the law cannot take hold of Him, 'made of a woman' will do us small pleasure. And He was so born, so 'made of a woman'. As the verity of His conception is in this 'made of a woman', so the purity is in this, that it is but 'of a woman', and no more; of the Virgin alone by the power of the Holy Ghost, without mixture of fleshly generation. By virtue whereof no original soil was in him. Just born He was, and 'no law for the just', no law could touch Him. And so we never the better for 'born of a woman'.

For if one be in debt and danger of the law, to have a brother of the same blood, made of the same woman, both as we say lying in the one belly, will little avail him, except he will also come 'under the law', that is, become his surety, and undertake for him. And such was our estate. As debtors we were by virtue of 'the handwriting that was against us'. Which was our bond, and we had forfeited it. And so, 'made of a woman', to us, without 'made under the Law', would have been to small purpose.

No remedy therefore, He must be new made; made again once more. And so He was, cast in a new mould; and at His second making 'made under the Law'; under which if He had not been made, we had been marred; even quite undone for ever, if this had not been done for us too. Therefore He became bound for us also, entered bond anew, took on Him not only our nature but our debt, our nature and condition both. Nature as men, condition as sinful men, expressed in the words following, 'them that were under the Law'; for that was our condition'. There had indeed been no capacity in Him to do this, if the former had not gone before, if He had not been as we 'made of a woman'. But the former was for this; 'made of a woman' He was, that He might be 'made under the Law': being 'of a woman'. He might then become 'under the

Law', which before he could not, but then He might and did; and so this still is the fuller. [. . .]

A time of fullness it will be, I know, in a sense; of fullness of bread, of fullness of bravery, of fullness of sport and pastime; and this it may be. And it hath been ever a joyful time in appearance, for it should be so. 'With the joy', saith Esay a verse or two before 'unto us a Child is born', 'that men rejoice with in harvest'. Not to go from our text here, with the joy of men that are come out of prison, have escaped the law; with the joy of men that have got the reversion of a goodly heritage. Only, that we forget not the principal; that this outward joy eat not up, evacuate not our spiritual joy proper to the feast; that we have in mind in the midst of our mirth the cause of it, Christ's sending, and the benefits that come thereby. And it shall be a good sign unto us if we can thus rejoice, if this our joy can be full, if we can make a spiritual blessing the object of our mirth. 'Blessed is the people that can rejoice on this manner'.

And after our joyfulness, or fullness of joy, our fullness of thanks of thankfulness, is to ensue; for with that fullness we are to celebrate it likewise. Our minds first, then our mouths, to be filled with blessing, and praise, and thanks to Him, That hath made our times not to fall into those empty ages of the world, but to fall within this 'fullness' of time', which 'so many Kings and Prophets desired to have lived in', but fell short of; and lived then when the times were full of shadows, and promises, and nothing else. How instantly they longed to have held such a feast, to have kept a Christmas, it is evident by David's 'Bow the Heavens', by Esay's 'Break the Heavens' and how much, I say, they longed for it; and therefore that we make not light account of it

To render our thanks then, and to remember to do it fully, to forget none; to Him that was sent, and to Him that 'sent'; 'sent His Son' in this, 'the Spirit of His Son' in the next verse. To begin with, it is the first duty enjoined us this day, to 'kiss the Babe', new born, That when His Father would send Him; said, 'Behold, I come' so readily; and when He would make Him, was content with 'Thou hast prepared for Me a body' to have a body made Him, meet for Him to suffer in; who willingly yielded to be our Shilo. [. . .]

And not to Him that was sent and made alone; but to the Father that sent Him, and to the Holy Ghost that made Him, as by Whom He was conceived. To the Father for His mission, the Son for His redemption, the Holy Ghost for His adoption; for by Him it is wrought. He that made Him Son of Man, doth likewise regenerate us to the state of the sons of God. And this for our thankfulness.

And to these two, to make the measure full, to join the fullness of duty, even whatsoever dutiful-minded persons may yield to a bountiful-minded and a bountiful-handed Benefactor. And with this to begin, to consecrate this first day of this fullness of time even with our service to Him at the full; which is then at the full when no part is missing; when all our duties of preaching, and praying, of hymns, of offering, of Sacrament and all, meet together. No fullness there is of our Liturgy or public solemn Service, without the Sacrament. Some part, yea the chief part is wanting, if that be wanting. But our thanks are surely not full without the Holy Eucharist, which is by interpretation, thanksgiving itself. Fully we cannot say, 'What reward shall I give unto the Lord?' but we must answer, 'we will take the Cup of salvation', and with it in our hands give thanks to Him, render Him our true Eucharist, or real thanksgiving indeed. In which Cup is the Blood not only of our redemption, of the covenant that freeth us from the Law and maketh the destroyer pass over us; but of our adoption, of the New Testament also which entitles us and conveys unto us, testament-wise or by way of legacy, the estate we have in the joy and bliss of His Heavenly Kingdom whereto we are adopted. We are then made partakers of Him, and with Him of both these His benefits. We there are made 'to drink of the Spirit', 'by which we are sealed to the day of our redemption' and adoption both. So that that our freeing from under the Law, our investiture into our new adopted state, are not fully consummate without it.

Nativity sermon 4, vol. 1, pp. 53–5, 61–3

Before James I at Whitehall, Christmas Day 1618

And this shall be a sign unto you; Ye shall find the Babe wrapped in swaddling clothes, lying in a manger.

Luke 2.12–14

Further meditation on the reality and humility of the Incarnation, emphasizing the lowliness of the 'cratch' – the manger. The word signatum is here retained: that which is marked or signified by the sign. 'Babe' in the Latin is infans, 'without speech'. T. S. Eliot took up the thought, 'The word within a word, unable to speak a word' in his poem 'Gerontion'.

From so poor a beginning He was able to advance so glorious a work. It was much from a babe floating in the flags of the Nilus in a basket of bulrushes, Moses, to gather himself a people, even the nation and king-dom of the Jews, and to deliver his law. It was infinitely much more from this Babe here lying in the cratch, to work the bringing in of the Gentiles, and the turning about of the whole world, and to publish His Gospel, 'the power of God to salvation'. Herein is power, from His cratch to do this. There to lay Him, and there lying to make so many nations come and adore Him, as since He hath. That if ever 'in His humility His judg-ment were exalted', if His 'power were ever made perfect in weakness', if ever He showed that 'God at the weakest is stronger than men in all their strength', 'in this sign it was'.

A sign, 'in that He casts from Him all outward signs and means, that He is of Himself all sufficient', 'and needs no power but His own.' His cratch and He will bring this work to pass. 'His glory on high, so much the higher for this.' Ever, but now more than ever, and in all His signs, but in this more glorious than in any, nay than in all them. And so 'this shall be the sign' shall be and should be for both.

But I waive all these, and say sixthly. Make of the sign what ye will, it skills not what it, be, never so mean. In the nature of a sign there is nothing but it may be such, all is in the thing signified. So it carry us to a rich *signatum* and worth the finding, what makes it a matter how mean the sign be? We are sent to a crib; not to an empty crib; Christ is in it. Be the sign never so simple, the *signatum* it carries us to makes amends. Any sign with such a *signatum*.

And I know not the man so squeamish but if, in his stable and under his manger, there were a treasure hid and he were sure of it, but thither he would, and pluck up the planks, and dig and rake for it, and be never a whit offended with the homeliness of the place. If then Christ be a treasure, as in Him are 'all the treasures of the wisdom and bounty of God', what skills it what be His sign? With this, with any other, Christ is worth the finding. Though the cratch be not worth the going to, Christ is worth the going for. He is not worthy of Christ that will not go any whither to find Christ.

Lastly, I would fain know why should the shepherds, why should any be ashamed of this sign? The Angels are not. 'No man proclaims or preaches of that, makes a hymn of that he is ashamed of'. And indeed, why should the Angels be ashamed to report it, seeing 'Christ is not ashamed' to wear it? And if He be not so to be found, never let us be so to find Him.

I conclude then. They that will have a Saviour without such a, sign, best stay for the Jews' Messias, or get them for their sign to somebody else. The Angel hath none, the Gospel knows none but this. We must take Christ as we find Him, cratch and all. The invention of the cratch and the invention of Christ fall both upon one feast – this day both: no severing of them. All which I trust by this show plainly, the sign was well assigned by the Angel. And so I hope we will not let the shepherds go alone, but go along with them too for company, to find Christ, 'by this sign.'

But the cratch is gone many years ago. What is our sign now? Why, what was this sign a sign of? There needs no straining at all – of humility clear; a humble sign, a sign of humility. Not always so, not with us where the highest minds will use the lowest signs; but with Christ, with such in whom is the mind of Christ there is no odds at all. Ye may strike, a tally between the sign and the *signatum*. Humility then: we shall find Him by that sign, where we find humility and not fail; and where that is not, be sure we shall never find Him. This day it is not possible to keep off of this theme; we cannot but we must fall upon it; it is so woven into every text there is no avoiding it. But of all, into the sign, most of all. Such a sign of such humility as never was.

Signs are taken for wonders. 'Master, we would fain see a sign', that is a miracle. And in this sense it is a sign to wonder at. Indeed, every word here is a wonder. An infant; the infant Word, the Word, without a word; the eternal Word not able to speak a word; a wonder sure. And swaddled; and that a wonder too. 'He that' (as in the thirty-eighth of Job He saith), 'taketh the vast body of the main sea, turns it to and fro, as a little child, and rolls it about with the swaddling bands of darkness'. He to come thus into clouts, Himself! But yet, all is well; all children are so. But 'in a manger', that is it, there is the wonder. Children lie not there; He doth. There lieth He, the Lord of glory without all glory. Instead of a palace, a poor stable; of a cradle of state, a beast's cratch; no pillow but a lock of hay; no hangings but dust and cobwebs; no attendants, but 'in the midst of animals', as the Fathers read the third of Habakkuk. For if the inn were full, the stable was not empty we may be sure. A sign this, nay three in one, able to amaze any.

And 'is it true?' saith Solomon, and makes a wonder of it: 'Will God accept a place in earth to receive Him?' when he had built Him a stately sumptuous Temple, and meant it by that. And is that a wonder if in such a Temple? What is it then, if in a corner of a stable, in a cratch there? Will He accept of that trow? If He will, 'this will be a sign' indeed. 'O Lord, O Lord', saith King David, his father, rapt with admiration, 'how wonderful!' What? Why? 'Thou madest Him lower than the Angels' – for to Christ doth the Apostle apply that verse 'lower than the Angels'. Nay, lower yet; saith Esay in his fifty-third, 'The lowest of men '. Nay, lower yet, saith the Angel here, lower than the lowest of men. For a stable, a cratch, is a place for beasts not for men. So low. Well may this be said a sign in this sense, to wonder at. If it be well looked into, it is able to strike any man into an ecstasy.

Nativity sermon 12, vol. 1, pp. 202–5

Before James I at Whitehall, Christmas Day 1613

Your father Abraham rejoiced to see my day.

John 8.56

This Nativity sermon begins with praise and joy for the sheer wonder of the celebration. The censure of Christians who do not respect and keep the feast takes note of Puritan objections to marking out any day except Sunday and anticipates the suppression of Christmas observance during the Commonwealth period.

Here is joy, joy at a sight, at the sight of a day, and that day Christ's. It is Christ that calleth it here, 'His day'; and no day so properly His, as His birthday. So the text comes full upon the day.

But to deduce it point by point.

First, Christ hath a day proper to Him, which in express terms He calleth here 'My day'.

Secondly, this day to be seen is a day of joy. Double joy; 'He rejoiced' and 'He was glad', both in the text.

And thirdly, which is somewhat strange, it was so to the Patriarch Abraham. Him we find here doing that which we now are about; seeing and rejoicing at the sight of Christ's day; taking notice of it, and taking joy in it.

Lastly, all this nothing displeasing to our Saviour Christ; for it is spoken by Him to the praise of Abraham that did it, and to the dislike of the Jews that did it not. To them is this speech; Christ tells them of Abraham's doing it, and blames them for not doing the like.

And what are we now disposing ourselves to do, but even the very same that is in the text here, to rejoice to see Christ's day?

And a three-fold warrant we have in this verse to do as we do. The Patriarch's doing it. Christ's allowance of the doing of it. And His dislike of the Jews for not doing it.

We have Abraham for our example; we do but as he did. In his time, Christ's day was a day of joy; and a day of joy is a feast, and so holden by him we see. Which falls out much to our content. For the same feasts, the same religion. So we find by this, that he and we are of one religion. One in substance, which is Christ; one in circumstance, which is His day. Christ Himself, Abraham's joy; nay, His day Abraham's joy too. The same 'My', that is, Christ; the same 'day', that is, Christmas.

Then, which is another degree, Abraham's example approved of by Christ, and that after somewhat a strange manner; for it is not here if you mark it, 'he rejoiced that he saw Me', but 'that he saw My day'. He makes His day the object of all this exultation and joy. His day, I say, and not Himself; commends Him, that He rejoiced at the sight not of Himself, but of it. Verily, this speech of His is much to the honour of His day; and the very solemnity of the feast, and all the joy and gladness thereon, may well be thought to have been founded upon this speech of His. Always, if 'he rejoiced that he saw' were a praise to Him; we may be sure, 'he rejoiced when he saw' can be no dispraise to us.

Add thirdly, Abraham's example approved by Christ. Not so approved as He leaves it at liberty, they that will may do the like; but that He reproves them that do it not. For He blames the Jews here for not doing herein as Abraham; 'Your father Abraham did it; you do it not'. Which is against them that have a spleen at this feast, that think they can joy in Him well enough, and set His day by; nay, and abrogate it quite; and in so doing they joy in Him all the better. Nay, love Him, love His feast. Joy not in it; nor in Him neither.

You shall see how they are mistaken. Therefore they do so they tell us, lest 'observing days and times' they should seem to Judaize. It falls out quite contrary. For who are they whom Christ here blameth? Are they not Jews? And wherefore blameth He them? For not doing as Abraham. And what did Abraham? Rejoice on His day. So upon the point it will fall out that not to rejoice on His day, that is indeed to Judaize, and they little better than these Jews that follow them in it.

Nay, here is another thing yet will grieve them more. Jews they shall be, but none of Abraham's children; no more than these were. Observe it well. It is the occasion of this speech, the very issue Christ Jesus takes with them. 'Our father Abraham' was still in their mouths; if, saith Christ, you were his children (mark that if), ye would follow your father; desire what he desired, and joy what he joyed in. Now, My day he so highly esteemed, as glad he was that he might see it; and you that would so fain father yourselves upon him are so far from that, as what he desired absent, ye despise present; what he would have been the better to see, ye are the worse that ye see it. Now then, how are these Abraham's children that have nothing of Abraham in them? Before, at the fortieth verse, 'Ye seek to kill Me for telling the truth. This did not Abraham', and ye do it. Here now again; 'He rejoiced in My day', and ye do it not. Do that he did not, do not that he did – how can these be Abraham's sons? Verily, as it is in Esay, 'Abraham would never know them for his'. None of his sons, these. Those are his sons that do as he did. And here now come in we. They Jews, but not Abraham's children; we Abraham's children, but not Jews; for as he did, so do we. There is joy with us at the sight of His day; we renew our joy so oft as by the revolution of the year it cometh about. And for this very point we find ourselves the nearer to Abraham, even for the joy of His day. Always sure we are, since Abraham did it, and Christ allowed it, and disallowed the contrary; by these three we have good warrant to do as we do. To make it a time of joy. And so, a time of joy God make it to us!

Nativity sermon 8, vol. 1, pp. 118–20

Before James I at Whitehall, Christmas Day 1622

We have seen His star in the East, and are come to worship Him.

Matthew 2.1–2

In the coming of the Magi he finds an example of acting in response to the call of faith. We too often pay only lip-service; and Andrewes makes an elaborate play on the Latin words in the Gospel: visimus, *'we have seen' and* venimus, *'we are come'. T. S. Eliot took the words following 'A cold coming they had of it' for the opening of his poem 'The Journey of the Magi'.*

Now to 'we are come', their coming itself. And it follows well. For it is not a star only, but a loadstar; and whither should His star lead? 'Whither lead us, but to Him Whose the star is?' The star to the star's Master.

All this while we have been at 'saying' and 'seeing'; now we come to 'doing', see them do somewhat upon It. It is not saying nor seeing will serve St James; he will call, and be still calling for 'show me thy faith by some work'. And well may he be allowed to call for it this day; it is the day of 'we have seen', appearing, being seen. You have seen His star, let

Him now see your star another while. And so they do. Make your faith to be seen; so it is – their faith in the steps of their faith. And so was Abraham's first by coming forth of his country; as these here do, and so 'walk in the steps of the faith of Abraham', do his first work.

It is not commended to stand gazing up to heaven too long; not on Christ Himself ascending, much less on His star. For they sat not still gazing on the star. Their 'we have seen' begat 'we are come'; their seeing made them come, but many a wild and weary step they made before they could come to say, 'Lo, here we are come'; come, and at our journey's end. To look a little on it. In this, their coming we consider, first the distance of the place they came from. It was not hard by as the shepherds, but a step to Bethlehem over the fields; this was riding many a hundred miles, and cost them many a day's journey. Secondly, we consider the way that they came, if it be pleasant, or plain and easy; for if it be, it is so much the better. This was nothing pleasant, for through deserts, all the way waste and desolate. Nor secondly, easy either; for over the rocks and crags of both Arabias, specially Petrea, their journey lay. Yet if safe – but it was not, but exceeding dangerous, as lying through the midst of the 'black tents, of Kedar', a nation of thieves and, cut-throats; to pass over the hills of robbers, infamous then and infamous to this day. No passing without great troop or convoy. Last we consider the time of their coming, the season of the year. It was no summer progress. A cold coming they had of it at this time of the year, just the worst time of the year to take a journey, and specially a long journey in. The ways deep, the weather sharp, the days short, the sun farthest off in 'the very dead of winter'. 'We are come,' if that be one, 'we are come', we are now come, come at this time, that sure is another.

And these difficulties they overcame, of a wearisome, irksome, troublesome, dangerous, unseasonable journey; and for all this they came. And came it, cheerfully and quickly, as appeareth by the speed they made. It was but 'we have seen', 'we are come', with them; 'they saw', and 'they came'; they no sooner saw, but they set out presently. So as upon the first appearing of the star, as it might be last night, they knew it was Balaam's star; it called them away, they made ready straight to begin their journey this morning. A sign they were highly conceited of His birth, believed some great matter of it, that they took all these pains, made all this haste that they might be there to worship Him with all the possible speed they could. Sorry for nothing so much as that they could not be there soon enough, with the very first, to do it even this day, the day of His birth. All considered, so there is more in 'we are come' than shows at the first sight. It was not for nothing it was said in the first verse, 'behold there came'; their coming hath a 'behold' on it, it well deserves it.

And we, what should we have done? Sure these men of the East shall rise in judgement against the men of the West, that is us, and their faith against ours in this point. With them it was but 'we have seen', 'we are come'; with us it would have been but 'we are coming' at most. Our fashion is, to see and see again, before we stir a foot, specially if it be to the worship of Christ. Come such a journey at such a time? No; but fairly have put it off to the spring of the year, till the days longer, and the ways fairer, and the weather warmer, till better traveling to Christ. Our Epiphany would sure have fallen in Easter-week at the soonest.

But then for the distance, desolateness, tediousness, and the rest, any of them were enough to mar our 'we are come' quite. It must be no great way, first, we must come; we love not that. Well fare the shepherds, yet they came but hard by; rather like them than the Magi. Nay, not like them neither. For with us the nearer, lightly the farther off; our proverb is you know, 'The nearer the Church, the farther from God'.

Nor it must not be through no desert, over no Petrea. If rugged or uneven the way, if the weather ill-disposed, if any never so little danger, it is enough to stay us. To Christ we cannot travel, but weather and way and all must be fair. If not, no journey, but sit still and see farther. As indeed all our religion is rather 'we have seen', contemplation, than 'we are come', a motion, or stirring to do aught.

But when we do it, we must be allowed leisure. Ever 'we are coming', never 'we are come'; ever coming, never come. We love to make no very great haste. To other things perhaps; not to 'worship' the place of the worship of God. Why should we? Christ is no wildcat. What talk ye of twelve days? And if it be forty days hence, ye shall be sure to find His Mother and Him; she cannot be churched till then. What needs such haste? The truth is, we conceit Him and His, birth but slenderly, and our haste, is even thereafter. But if we be at that point, we must be out of this 'we are come'; they like enough to leave us behind. Best get us a new Christmas in September we are not like to come to Christ at this feast. Enough for 'we are come'.

Nativity sermon 15, vol. 1, pp. 256–8

3

Passion, Resurrection and Ascension

At the Court, Good Friday, 25 March 1597

And they shall look upon Me whom they have pierced.

Zechariah 12.10

In this, the first of his Sermons on the Passion, Andrewes urges us to be drawn to repentance by feeling deeply with the suffering of Christ. Josias: Josiah, King of Judah, killed at the battle of Megiddo 609 BC.

Looking upon Him, we may bring forth for the first effect that which immediately followeth this text itself in this text, 'And they mourned Him' – 'Look and mourn' First, 'look and lament', or mourn; which is indeed the most kindly and natural effect of such a spectacle. 'Look upon Him that is pierced', and with looking upon Him be pierced thyself; 'look and be pierced'. A good effect of our first look, if we could bring it forth. At leastwise, if we cannot 'look and be pierced', yet that it might be 'look and be wounded', 'that with looking on Him we might be pricked in our hearts', and have it enter past the skin, though it go not clean through. Which difference in this verse the Prophet seemeth to insinuate, when first he willeth us to mourn as for one's only son, with whom all is lost. Or, if that cannot be had, to mourn as for a first-begotten son, which is though not so great, yet a great mourning; even for the first-begotten, though other sons be left.

And, in the next verse, if we cannot reach to natural grief, yet he wisheth us to mourn with a civil; even with such a lamentation as was made for Josias. And behold a greater than Josias is here. Coming not, as he, to an honourable death in battle, but to a most vile death, the death of a malefactor; and not, as Josias, dying without any fault of theirs, but mangled and massacred in this shameful sort for us, even for us and our transgressions. Verily, the dumb and senseless creatures had this effect wrought in them, of mourning at the sight of His death; in their kind sorrowing for the murder of the Son of God. And we truly shall be much more senseless than they, if it have in us no work to the like effect. Especially, considering it was not for them He suffered all this, nor they no profit by it, but for us it was, and we by it saved; and yet they had compassion, and we none. Be this then the first.

Now, as the first is 'look upon Him and be pierced'; so the second may be, and that fitly, 'look upon Him and pierce'; and pierce that in thee that was the cause of Christ's piercing, that is, sin and the lusts thereof. For as men that are pierced indeed with the grief of an indignity offered, withal are pricked to take revenge on him that offers it, such a like affection ought our second looking to kindle in us, even to take a wreak or revenge upon sin, 'because it hath been the cause of all this'. I mean, as the Holy Ghost termeth it, a mortifying or crucifying; a thrusting through of our wicked passions and concupiscences, in some kind of repaying those manifold villainies, which the Son of God suffered by means of them. At leastwise, as before, if it kindle not our zeal so far against sin, yet that it may slake our zeal and affection to sin; that is, 'look upon Christ lest you look upon sin'. That we have less mind, less liking, less acquaintance with sin, for the Passion-sake. For that by this means we do in some sort spare Christ, and at least make His wounds no wider; whereas by affecting sin anew we do what in us lieth to crucify Him afresh, and both increase the number, and, enlarge the wideness of His wounds.

It is no unreasonable request, that if we list not wound sin, yet seeing Christ hath wounds enough, and they wide and deep enough, we should forbear to pierce Him farther, and have at least this second fruit of our looking upon Him; either to look and to pierce sin, or to look and spare to pierce Him any more.

Now, as it was sin that gave Him these wounds, so it was love to us that made Him receive them, being otherwise able enough to have avoided them all. So that He was pierced with love no less than with grief, and it was that wound of love made Him so constantly to endure all the other. Which love we may read in the palms of His hands, as the Fathers express it out of Isaiah; for 'in the palms of His hands He hath graven us', that He might not forget us. And the print of the nails in them, are as capital letters to record His love towards us. For Christ pierced on the cross is 'the very book of love' laid open before us. And again, this love of His we may read in the cleft of His heart. St Bernard saith, 'the point of the spear serves us instead of a key, letting us through His wounds see His very bowels', the bowels of tender love and most keen compassion, that would for us endure to be so entreated. That if the Jews that stood by said truly of Him at Lazarus' grave, 'Behold, how He loved him!'

when He shed a few tears out of His eyes; much more truly may we say of Him, 'Behold how He loved us!' seeing Him shed both water and blood, and that in great plenty, and that out of His heart.

Which sight ought to pierce us with love too, no less than before it did with sorrow. With one, or with both, for both have power to pierce; but specially love, which except it had entered first and pierced Him, no nail or spear could ever have entered. Then let this be the third, 'look and be pierced with love of Him' that so loved thee, that He gave Himself in this sort to be pierced for thee.

Passion sermon 1, vol. 2, pp. 130–32

Before James I at Whitehall, Good Friday, 6 April 1604

Behold, and see if there be any sorrow like unto My sorrow, which is done unto Me.

Lamentations 1.12

This powerful devotional reflection on Good Friday tends towards a penal interpretation of the Atonement. It is a fine example of how Andrewes can make his point by frequent repetition of a word or phrase – in this sermon it is 'regard', his rendering of 'behold'.

Yes sure, His complaint is just, 'Have ye no regard?' None? And yet never the like? None? And it pertains unto you? 'No regard?' As if it were some common ordinary matter, and the like never was? 'No regard?' As if it concerned you not a whit, and it toucheth you so near? As if He should say, Rare things you regard, yea, though they no ways pertain to you: this is exceeding rare, and will you not regard it? Again, things that nearly touch you you regard, though they be not rare at all: this toucheth you exceeding near, even as near as your soul toucheth you, and will you not yet regard it? Will neither of these by itself move you? Will not both these together move you? What will move you? Will pity? Here is distress never the like. Will duty? Here is a Person never the like. Will fear? Here is wrath never the like. Will remorse? Here is sin never the like. Will kindness? Here is love never the like. Will bounty? Here are benefits never the like. Will all these? Here they be all, all above any like unto them, all in the highest degree.

Truly the complaint is just, it may move us; it wanteth no reason, it may move; and it wanteth no affection in the delivery of it to us, on His part to move us. Sure it moved Him exceeding much; for among all the deadly sorrows of His most bitter Passion, this, even this, seemeth to be His greatest of all, and that which did most affect Him, even the grief of the slender reckoning most men have it in; as little respecting Him, as if He had done or suffered nothing at all for them. For of all the sharp pains He endureth He complaineth not, but of this He complaineth, of no regard; that which grieveth Him most, that which most He moaneth is this. It is strange He should be in pains, such pains as never any was, and not complain Himself of them, but of want of regard only. Strange, He should not make request, O deliver Me, or relieve Me! But only, O consider and regard Me! In effect as if He said, None, no deliverance, no relief do I seek; regard I seek. And all that I suffer, I am content with it, I regard it not, I suffer most willingly, if this I may find at your hands, regard.

Truly, this so passionate a complaint may move us, it moved all but us; for most strange of all it is, that all the creatures in Heaven and earth seemed to hear this His mournful complaint, and in their kind to show their regard of it. The sun in Heaven shrinking in his light, the earth trembling under it, the very stones cleaving in sunder, as if they had sense and sympathy of it, and sinful men only not moved with it. And yet it was not for the creatures this was done to Him, to them it per-taineth not; but for us it was, and to us it doth. And shall we not yet regard it? shall the creature, and not we? shall we not?

If we do not, it may appertain to us, but we pertain not to it; it pertains to all but all pertain not to it. None pertain to it but they that take benefit by it; and none take benefit by it no more than by the brazen serpent, but they that fix their eye on it. Behold, consider, and regard it; the profit, the benefit is lost without regard.

If we do not, as this was a day of God's 'fierce wrath' against Him, only for regarding us; so there is another day coming, and it will quickly be here, a day of like 'fierce wrath' against us, for not regarding Him. 'And who regardeth the power of His wrath?' He that doth, will surely regard this.

In that day, there is not the most careless of us all but shall cry as they did in the Gospel, 'Pertains it not to Thee, carest Thou not that we perish?' Then would we be glad to pertain to Him and His Passion. Pertains it to us then, and pertains it not now? Sure now it must, if then it shall.

Then to give end to this complaint, let us grant Him His request, and regard His Passion. Let the rareness of it, the nearness to us, let pity or duty, fear or remorse, love or bounty; any of them or all of them; let the justness of His complaint, let His affectionate manner of complaining of this and only this, let the shame of the creatures' regard, let our profit or our peril, let something prevail with us to have it in some regard.

Some regard! Verily, as His sufferings, His love, our good by them are, so should our regard be a 'not like unto' too; that is, a regard of these, and of nothing in comparison of these. It should be so, for with the benefit ever the regard should arise.

But God help us poor sinners, and be merciful unto us! Our regard is a 'not like unto' indeed, but it is backward, and in a contrary sense; that is, nowhere so shallow, so short, or so soon done. It should be otherwise, it should have our deepest consideration this, and our highest regard.

But if that cannot be had, our nature is so heavy, and flesh and blood so dull of apprehension in spiritual things, yet at leastwise some regard. Some I say; the more the better, but in any wise some, and not as here no regard, none at all. Some ways to show we make account of it, to withdraw ourselves, to void our minds of other matters, to set this before us, to think upon it, to thank Him for it, to regard Him and stay and see whether He will regard us or no. Sure He will, and we shall feel our 'hearts pricked' with sorrow by consideration of the cause in us – our sin; and again, 'warm within us', by consideration of the cause in Him – His love; till by some motion of grace He answer us, and show that our regard is accepted of Him.

And this, as at all other times, for no day is amiss but at all times some time to be taken for this duty, so specially on this day; this day, which we hold holy to the memory of His Passion, this day to do it; to make this day, the day of God's wrath and Christ's suffering, a day to us of serious consecration and regard of them both.

It is kindly to consider 'the work of the day in the day it was wrought'; and this day it was wrought. The day therefore, whatsoever business be, to lay them aside a little; whatsoever our haste, yet to stay a little, and to spend a few thoughts in calling to mind and taking to regard what this day the Son of God did and suffered for us; and all for this end, that what He was then we might not be, and what He is now we might be for ever.

Which Almighty God grant we may do, more or less, every one of us, according to the several measures of His Grace in us!

Passion sermon 2, vol. 2, pp. 154–7

Before James I at Whitehall, Easter Day 1608

They came unto the sepulchre.

Mark 16.1–7

What may seem at first sight to be patronizing is in fact a remarkable insight for the period, which praises the fidelity of the women and honours their witness to the Resurrection.

As the text lieth, the part that first offereth itself, is the parties to whom the message came. Which were three women. Where, finding that women were the first that had notice of Christ's resurrection, we stay. For it may seem strange that passing by all men, yea the Apostles themselves, Christ would have His resurrection first of all made known to that sex. Reasons are rendered, of divers diversely. We may be bold to allege that the Angel doth in the text, 'Whom do you seek?' for they sought Christ. And Christ 'is not unrighteous to forget the work and labour of their love' that seek Him. Verily there will appear more love and labour in these women, than in men, even the Apostles themselves. At this time, I know not how, men were then become women and did 'bear female spirits', and women were men. Sure the more manly of the twain. The Apostles, they sat mured up, all 'the doors fast' about them; sought not, went not to the sepulchre. Neither Peter that loved Him, nor John whom He loved, till these women brought them word. But these women we see were last at His Passion, and first at His Resurrection; stayed longest at that, came soonest to this, even in this respect to be respected. Sure, as it is said of the Law, 'It hastens not to those who sleep but to those who are awake', so may it no less truly be said of the Gospel. We see it here, it cometh not to sleepers, but to them that are awake, and up and about their business, as these women were. So that there was a capacity in them to receive this prerogative.

Before I leave this part of the parties, I may not omit to observe Mary Magdalene's place and precedence among the three. All the Fathers are careful to note it. That she standeth first of them, for it seemeth no good order. She had had seven devils in her, as we find. She had had the blemish to be called 'a woman who was a sinner', as one famous and notorious in that kind. The others were of honest report, and never so stained, yet is she named with them. With them were much, but not only with them, but before them. With them; and that is to show Christ's resurrection, as well as His death, reacheth to sinners of both sexes; and that, to sinners of note, no less than those that seem not to have greatly gone astray; but before them too, and that is indeed to be noted; that she is the first in the list of women, and St Peter in that of men. These two, the two chief sinners, either of their sex. Yet they, the two, whose lots came first in partaking this news. And this to show that chief sinners as these were, if they carry themselves as they did, shall be at no loss by their fall; shall not only be pardoned but honoured even as he was, like these, with 'the first robe' in all the wardrobe, and stand foremost of all.

Resurrection sermon 3, vol. 2, pp. 223–4

Before James I at Whitehall, Easter Day, 16 April 1620

She, supposing him to be the gardener.

John 20.11–17

Mary Magdalene's mistake led her to the truth. When we seek Christ, He is with us and guides us to find Him even as we seek.

Augustine saith, 'Christ is found, found by her; and this case of hers shall be the case of all that seriously seek Him'. This woman here for one, she sought Him we see. They that went to Emmaus to-day, they but talked on Him sadly, and they both found Him. Why, He is found of them that seek Him not; but of them that seek Him, never but found. 'For Thou Lord never failest them that seek Thee'. 'God is not unrighteous to forget the work and labour of their love that seek Him'.

So find Him they shall, but happily not all so fully at first, no more than she did. For first, to try her yet a little farther, He comes unknown, stands by her, and she little thought it had been He.

A case that likewise falls out full oft. Doubtless, 'He is not far from every one of us', saith the Apostle to the Athenians. But He is nearer us many times than we think; even hard by us and we not aware of it, saith Job. And 'O if we did know', and it standeth us in hand to pray that we may know when He is so, for that is 'the time of our visitation'.

St John saith here, the Angels were sitting; St Luke saith, they stood. They are thus reconciled. That Christ coming in presence, the Angels which before were sitting stood up. Their standing up made Mary Magdalene turn her to see who it was they rose to. And so Christ she saw, but knew Him not.

Not only not knew Him, but mis-knew Him, took Him for the

gardener. Tears will dim the sight, and it was not yet scarce day, and she seeing one, and not knowing what any one should make in the ground so early but he that dressed it, she might well mistake. But it was more than so; her eyes were not holden only that she did not know Him, but over and beside He did appear 'in another form', in some such shape as might resemble the gardener whom she took Him for.

Proper enough it was, it fitted well the time and place, this person. The time, it was the spring; the place, it was the garden: that place is most in request at that time, for that place and time a gardener doth well.

Of which her so taking Him, St Gregory saith well, 'proceeding in mistaking, she was not mistaken'. She did not mistake in taking Him for a gardener; though she might seem to err in some sense, yet in some other she was in the right. For in a sense, and a good sense, Christ may well be said to be a gardener, and indeed is one. For our rule is, Christ as He appears, so He is ever; no false semblant in Him.

A gardener He is then. The first, the fairest garden that ever was, Paradise, He was the gardener, it was of His planting. So, a gardener.

And ever since it is He That as God makes all our gardens green, sends us yearly the spring, and all the herbs and flowers we then gather; and neither Paul with his planting, nor Apollos with his watering, could do any good without Him. So a gardener in that sense.

But not in that alone; but He it is that gardens our 'souls' too, and makes them, as the Prophet saith, 'like a well-watered garden'; weeds out of them whatsoever is noisome or unsavory, sows and plants them with true roots and seeds of righteousness, waters them with the dew of His grace, and makes them bring forth fruit to eternal life.

But it is none of all these, but besides all these, nay over and above all these, this day if ever, most properly He was a gardener. Was one, and so after a more peculiar manner might take this likeness on Him. Christ rising was indeed a gardener, and that a strange one, Who made such an herb grow out of the ground this day as the like was never seen before, a dead body to shoot forth alive out of the grave.

I ask, was He so this day alone? No, but this profession of His, this day begun, He will follow to the end. For He it is That by virtue of this morning's act shall garden our bodies too, turn all our graves into garden plots; yea, shall one day turn land and sea and all into a great garden, and so husband them as they shall in due time bring forth live bodies, even all our bodies alive again.

Long before, did Esay see this and sing of it in his song, resembling the resurrection to a spring garden. 'Awake and sing', saith he; 'ye that dwell for a time are as it were sown in the dust, for His dew shall be as the dew of herbs, and the earth shall shoot forth her dead'. So then, He appeared no other than He was; a gardener He was, not in show alone, but 'in deed and truth', and so came in His own likeness. This for Christ's appearing. Now to His speech, but as unknown still.

'Jesus saith to her, Woman, why weepest thou? whom seekest thou?' She, supposing He had been the gardener, said to Him, 'Sir, if thou have borne Him hence, tell me where thou hast laid Him, and I will take Him thence'.

Still she weeps; so He begins with 'Why weepest thou?' asks the same questions the Angels had before; only quickens it a little with 'whom seek you?' So, Whom she sought, He asks her 'Whom she sought'. Augustine saith, 'If she seek Him, why knows she Him not? If she know Him, why seeks she Him still?' A common thing with us, this also; to seek a thing, and when we have found it, not to know we have it so, but even 'to ask Christ for Christ'. Which however it fall in other matters, in this seeking of Christ it is safe. Even when we seek Christ, to pray to Christ to help us to find Christ; we shall do it full evil without Him.

Resurrection sermon 14, vol. 3, pp. 14–17

Before James I at Whitehall, Easter Day, 21 April 1622

Go to My brethren.

John 20.17

The Gospel begins on the day of the Resurrection and is completed at the Ascension. Mary Magdalene is regarded as numbered among the Apostles. Andrewes identifies her with the woman with the ointment, who is named in this Gospel as Mary of Bethany. As so often, he urges an active response to the Gospel, witness rather than passive adoration.

Well, when she comes to His brethren, what then? 'And say to them', or tell them. By which words 'say to them' He gives her a commission. 'Go' is her mission, 'tell them' her commission. A commission, to publish the first news of His rising, and as it falls out, of His ascending too.

The Fathers say that by this word she was by Christ made an Apostle, nay, 'an Apostle to the Apostles themselves.'

An Apostle; for what lacks she? Sent first, immediately from Christ Himself; and what is an Apostle but so? Secondly, sent to declare and make known; and what difference between 'Go and preach', and 'Go and tell', but only the number? The thing is the same. And last, what was she to make known? Christ's rising and ascending. And what are they but 'the Gospel', yea the very Gospel of the Gospel?

This day, with Christ's rising, begins the Gospel; not before. Crucified, dead and buried, no good news, no Gospel they in themselves. And them the Jews believe as well as we. The first Gospel of all is the Gospel of this day, and the Gospel of this day is this Mary Magdalene's Gospel, 'the prime Gospel' of all, before any of the other four. That Christ is risen and upon His ascending, and she the first that ever brought these glad tidings. At her hands the Apostles themselves received it first, and from them we all.

Which, as it was a special honour, and 'wheresoever this Gospel is preached, shall be told for a memorial of her', so was it withal, not without some kind of enthwiting to them, to the Apostles, for sitting at home so drooping in a corner, that Christ not finding any of them is fain to seek Him a new Apostle; and finding her where He should have found them and did not, to send by the hand of her that He first found at the sepulchre's side, and to make Himself a new Apostle, And send her to them, to enter them as it were, and catechize them in the two Articles of the Christian Faith, the Resurrection and Ascension of Christ. To her, they and we both owe them, the first notice of them.

And by this, lo, the amends we spake of is made her for her 'Do not touch Me', full amends. For to be thus sent, to be the messenger of these so blessed tidings, is a higher honour, a more special favour done here, a better good turn, every way better than if she had been let alone, had her desire, touched Christ, which she so longed for, and so eagerly reached at. Better sure, for I reason thus. Christ, we may be sure, would never have enjoined her to leave the better, to take the worse; to leave to touch Him, to go to tell them, if to go to tell them had not been the better.

So that hence we infer, that to go and carry comfort to them that need it, to tell them of Christ's rising that do not know it, is better than to tarry and do nothing but stand touching Christ. Touching Christ gives place to teaching Christ. 'Go and tell' better than 'stay and touch'. Christ we see is for 'go and tell'. That if we were in case where we might touch Christ, we were to leave Christ untouched, and even to give ourselves a 'do not touch Me', to go and do this; and to think ourselves better employed in telling them, than in touching Him.

Will you observe withal how well this agrees with her offer a little before of 'I will carry Him'? She must needs know of the gardener, 'Tell me where you have laid Him', and she 'would take Him and carry Him', that she would. Why, you that would so fain take and carry Me being dead, go take and carry Me now alive; that is, carry news that I am alive, and yon shall better please Me with this 'I will carry Him' a great deal; it shall be a better carrying, 'I will carry Him' in a better sense than ever was that. Stand not here then touching Me, go and touch them; and with the very touch of this report you shall work in them a kind of that you see in Me, a kind of resurrection from a doleful and dead, to a cheerful and lively estate.

'Tell them' what? 'Tell them that I ascend', that is, am about to ascend, am upon the point of it, am very shortly to do it. 'That that is near done, we reckon as good as done'.

'Tell them that I ascend'. Why, how now, what day is to day? It is not Ascension day; it is Easter, and but early Easter yet. His ascension is forty days off. This were a text for that day. Why speaks He of that now? Why not rather, tell them that I am risen – more proper for this day? Why, He needs not tell her that, she could tell that of herself, she saw it. And besides, in saying 'I ascend', He implies fully as much. Till He be risen, ascend He cannot; He must ascend out of the grave ere He can ascend up to Heaven, 'He is risen' must be past ere 'I ascend' can come. 'I ascend' then puts His resurrection past all peradventure; He needs say no more of that, of his rising. But as she saw by His rising that He had 'the keys of hell and death', and unlocked those doors and came out from thence; so by 'I ascend' He tells her farther that He hath the keys of Heaven-gates also, which He would now unlock, and so set open the kingdom of Heaven to all believers.

Resurrection sermon 16, vol. 3, pp. 44–6

Before James I at Whitehall, Easter Day 1608

If any man seem to be contentious, we have no such custom, neither the Churches of God.

1 Corinthians 11.16

Exaltation of Easter Day and its Eucharist combined with reference to escape from the Gunpowder and Gowrie plots. A further attack on those who would honour only the Sabbaths and not the great festivals.

The Lord's Day hath testimony in Scripture – I insist upon that; that

Easter-day must needs be as ancient as it. For how came it to be 'the Lord's Day', but that as it is in the Psalm 'the Lord made it'? And why made He it? But because on it 'the Stone cast aside', that is Christ, was made the 'Head-stone of the corner'? That is, because then the Lord rose, because His resurrection fell upon it?

Now what a thing were it, that all the Sundays in the year that are but abstracts, as it were, of this day, the very day of the Resurrection, that they should be kept; and this day, the day itself, the prototype and archetype of them all, should not be kept, but laid aside quite, and be clean forgotten? That the day in the week we should keep; and the day of the month itself, and return of the year, we should not keep? Even of very congruity it is to be as they, and somewhat more.

Take example by ourselves. For his Majesty's deliverance the fifth of August; for his Majesty's, and ours, the fifth of November, being Tuesday both; for these a kind of remembrance we keep, one Tuesday every week in the year. But when by course of the year in their several months, the very original days themselves come about; shall we not, do we not celebrate them in much more solemn manner? What question is there? weigh them well, you will find the case alike. One cannot be, but the other also must be Apostolic.

For the last proof I have yet reserved one; or rather, three in one. The custom of Baptism, known to have been ministered as upon that day, all the primitive Church through. A thing so known, as their Homilies on Baptism were most upon that day. St Basil I name. In his upon Easter-day, he shows the custom of baptizing then, and the reason of it.

The use of the keys, at that time specially. Then were the censures inflicted; then were they released. Inflicted. Against that time, did St Paul cut off the incestuous person, that a little leaven might not sour them all. Even against the time that 'Christ our Passover was offered, and they therefore to hold this feast'. Released. So you shall find the Council of Ancyra, elder than that of Nicea, order, the censures should determine all, endure no longer 'than the great day' – so in their common speech they termed Easter, and then all to be restored. To which purpose the Council of Nicea took order, there should be in Lent a Synod yearly to this end; that by it all quarrels being taken up, and all things set straight, they might be in better case to come with their oblation at Easter to the Sacrament.

And last, by the never broken custom of a solemn Eucharist, ever upon this day. Origen in his seventh upon Exodus, he saith, our Easter-day far passeth the Jewish Easter. They had no manna on theirs – the Passover was eaten in Egypt, manna came not till they were in the wilderness – but we, saith he, we never keep our Passover, but we are sure of manna upon it, the true Manna, 'the Bread of life that came down from Heaven'. For they had no Easter then without a Communion.

Resurrection sermon 13, vol. 2, pp 426–7

Before James I at Greenwich, Whitsunday, 12 June 1614

Thou hast ascended on high, thou hast led captivity captive.

Psalm 68.18

A joyful commemoration of the Ascension. The mention of new sea passages and the commercial metaphors reflect the enthusiasm of the period for trade and discovery.

'Thou art gone up' – a motion; and 'on high' – a place. Christ in His ascendant going up, Christ 'on high' is a good sight. A better sight to see Him so, 'an eagle in the clouds than a worm in the dust', as a great while we did. To see 'a cloud to receive Him' than a gravestone to cover Him. Better 'leading captivity' than Himself led captive. Better 'receiving gifts for men' than receiving wrong from them. Yet it is strange, St Paul commenting on this verse whereto we shall often have recourse as we are looking at 'His going up on high', pulls us back and tells us of His being here down below: 'In that He ascended', what is it, saith he, but that He descended first? A note out of season one would think. But he best knew what was proper and pertinent, and that is, that Christ's going up is 'ascending after descending'.

And this, as it is for His glory – for when one hath been down, then to get up is twice to get up – far more for His glory than if He never had been down. And the lower He hath been down, the more glorious is His getting up. 'Being overcome to overcome is twice to overcome', for so he overcomes his overcomers, and that is a double victory. As for His glory, so for our good. For His being above before He was below, is nothing to us. But being below first, and then that He went up, that is it we hold by. As the Son of God He came down, as the Son of man He went up. If as the Son of man, there is hope that the sons of men may do the like.

But always remember there must be a descent before. 'The angel rose up and became a devil'. Why? He never descended first, and therefore is now in the bottom of hell. But He That first descended, and ascended after, is now in the top of Heaven. To teach us this high top must have a deep root. He that is thus high now, was once low enough. We to be as He was, before we be as He is. Descending by humility, condescending by charity. For he that so descends with Him, he it is and none other that shall ascend up after Him. This is St Paul upon 'Thou hast gone up', His motion.

Now, will you hear him upon 'on high', the pitch of his motion? 'On high' is somewhat a doubtful term: if it be but to some high mountain, as they thought of Elias, it is 'on high', that. How high then? The Apostle takes the true altitude for us. Neither to Sion, nor to Sinai: set one upon the other, and Pelion upon Ossa too, it is higher yet. So high, saith St Luke, 'till a cloud came and took Him out of their sight'. And what became of Him then? That the Apostle supplies. He came 'above', 'aloft'; 'above all the heavens', even the very highest of them.

Keeping just correspondence between his high and his low. That was to the 'lowest parts of the earth', than which none lower, none beneath them. This was 'the highest top of the heavens', than which none higher, none above them.

So, 'Let God arise', the first verse is not enough; that was but from the lower parts of the earth to the upper parts of it. 'Let Him go up on high'; 'Set up Thyself, O Lord, above the heavens' – there is His right place. And so now He is where He should be. This for 'on high'.

But we must not stand taking altitudes; this is but the gaze of the Ascension. The Angels blamed the Apostles; that blame will fall upon us, if we make but a gaze of it. What is there in it 'for us men'?

First, is He 'gone up on high'? We may be sure then all is done and dispatched here below. He would not hence, till His errand were done He came for. All is dispatched – for look to the text; He went not up till the battle fought, and the victory gotten. For the next point is, 'Captivity is led captive'. So no more for Him here to do; 'it is finished'. And after it was 'it is finished' for us, no reason but it should be 'I have finished' with Him also.

But though all be done here, all is not there; there above, whither He is gone. There is somewhat still to be done for us. We have our cause there to be handled, and to be handled against a false and slanderous adversary – so Job found him. By means of His being there 'on high', saith St John, 'we have an Advocate' will see it take no harm. And what were such an one worth in place there!

But as our case is, for the most part, we rather stand in need of a good High Priest to make intercession, than of a ready Advocate to put in a plea for us. And He is there likewise to that end; 'on high' within the 'holy of holies', as 'a faithful High Priest' for ever to appear, and to make an atonement with God for our transgressions. Thus there all is well.

But how shall we do here, if He be gone up 'on high' from us? Not a whit worse. 'Who rideth upon the heaven in thy help', saith Moses. By being there He is the better able to help us, to help us against our enemies. For in that He is 'on high', He hath the vantage of the high ground; and so able to annoy them, to strike them down, and lay them flat – St Paul found it; yea to 'rain down fire and brimstone, storm and tempest, upon them'.

To help us against our wants. Wants both temporal, for from 'on high' He can 'send down a gracious rain upon His inheritance', to refresh it; and spiritual, for from 'on high' He did send down the gifts and graces of the Spirit, the 'gifts He gave' of this feast, and of this text both. Look to the text. He is so gone up that our enemies are his captives: we shall not need to fear, they can go no farther than their chain. And though He be gone, 'He gave gifts', He is ready to supply us upon our need with all gifts requisite. We shall not need to want; for no good thing will He withhold from them that have their hearts upon Him and upon His ascension; that lift up their hearts to Him there.

There is yet one, and I keep that, for it shall be the last. In that He is ascended into Heaven, Heaven is to be ascended to; 'by the new and living way that is prepared through the veil of His flesh', a passage there lieth thither. They talk of discoveries, and much ado is made of a new passage found out to this or that place: what say you to this discovery 'on high', this passage into the 'land of the living'? Sure it passes all. And this discovery is here, and upon this discovery there is begun a commerce, or trade of intercourse, between Heaven and us. The commodities whereof are these gifts, we shall after deal with them, and a kind of agency; Christ being there for us, and the Spirit here for God; either, agent for other. It is the happiest news this, that ever came to mankind.

Whitsun sermon 7, vol. 3, pp 223–6

4

The Holy Spirit

Before James I at Whitehall, Whitsunday, 31 May 1612

Have ye received the Holy Ghost since ye believed? And they said unto him, We have not so much as heard whether there be any Holy Ghost.

Acts 19.1–3

This long extract is an example of the deep importance of the Holy Spirit in the theology of Andrewes. He expounds the place of the Holy Spirit in the Trinity, and to understand his thought two Latin words are retained: unum *refers to the unity of the Godhead, while the denial of* unus *defends the distinctiveness of the Persons. He makes a strong appeal to the treatise 'Of the Holy Spirit' by Basil of Cappadocia. He maintains the* filioque *clause in the Nicene Creed – that the Spirit proceeds from the Father and the Son, a point that has been one of the matters of dispute between the eastern and western Churches. He touches on the* theosis *that is often stated or implied in his sermons. He ends by declaring our need of the Holy Spirit to confirm and strengthen the hearing of the word and to be received in the Eucharist.*

The hearing of Him first; then the receiving of Him. The hearing, and therein where we shall hear of Him; and what we shall hear of Him. Where we shall hear of Him at our baptism. And what we shall hear of Him there; that one there is at least, and I trust somewhat else besides.

Then the receiving of Him. And in it three points: First, that this question must be answered too, and so we bound to receive Him. And that either *affirmative* or *negative*. We have, or we have not. Then, have we received Him? How to know if we have. Have we not received Him? How to procure, if we have not. In the former, of hearing, is matter of faith. In the latter, of receiving, matter of moral duty. Both meet to be entreated of at all times; but at no time so fit and so proper, as at this feast.

There is no receiving of Him that is not. Therefore no talk of receiving, no place for the first question, 'Have ye received?' till the latter be first resolved, Is there one to receive? For resolution whereof he might have sent them to the very beginning of Genesis, where they should have heard, 'the Spirit of God moved on the face of the waters'. Or to the law, where the same Spirit came down upon the seventy elders. Or to the Psalms, where they should have heard David say of Him, 'send forth Thy Spirit and all shall be made'. And 'take not Thy Holy Spirit from me'. Or to the Prophets – the Prophet Esay, Christ's first text, 'The Spirit of God is upon me'. The Prophet Joel, St Peter's text this day, 'I will pour My Spirit upon all flesh'.

Or if ever they had heard of our Saviour Christ, St Paul might have sent them to His conception, where they should have heard the angel say, 'The Holy Spirit will come upon thee' to the Blessed Virgin. To Christ's baptism, where He came upon Christ in a visible shape. To His promise so often iterate, of sending them 'the Holy Ghost'. To His caveat 'not to sin against the Holy Ghost' in any wise; it was a high and heinous offence, it could not be remitted.

Or if they had heard of the Apostles, of Christ's breathing on them, and willing them to 'receive the Holy Ghost'. Or but of this day, and in what sort He was visibly sent down, like fiery tongues, upon each of them. Or of their solemn meeting and council at Jerusalem, and decrees there, the tenor whereof was, 'it seemed good to the Holy Ghost and us'. Or but of the strange end that happened to Ananias, they could not choose but have heard his offence told him by Saint Peter, 'he had lied to the Holy Ghost'; and straight upon it, 'he had not lied to man, but to God' directly.

All this he might, yet this he did not, but takes a plain course, sends them to their baptism, still supposing it to be Christ's baptism they were baptized with, the only true baptism. And, seeing the Apostle upon good advice took that for the best way, we cannot follow a better direction; and so, let us take it. We mean not, I trust, to renounce our baptism. By it we are that we are. And at it we shall not fail but hear, There is a Holy Ghost. Express mention of Him is directly given in charge in the set form of baptism prescribed by our Saviour, that all should be, as we all are, baptized 'in the Name of the Father, the Son, and the Holy Ghost'.

Yea, I add further; he could no better refer them than to baptism. For a special prerogative hath the Holy Ghost in our baptism, above the other two Persons. That 'laver', is His 'laver' properly; where, we are not only to be baptized into Him, as into the other two, but also, even to be baptized with Him, which is proper to Him alone. For, besides the water, we are there, to be 'born anew of the Holy Ghost' also, else is there 'no entering for us into the kingdom of God'.

This for baptism. But let me also tell you a saying – it is St Basil's, and well worth your remembering. He beginneth with, 'In Him we are baptized', and proceedeth three degrees further, all rising from thence naturally; they be but the train of baptism.

First. 'As we are baptized, so we believe'. As is our baptism, so is our belief. And our belief is there, at our baptism, repeated from point to point. A point whereof is, 'I believe in the Holy Ghost'. And we desire to be baptized in that faith. There He is now again, at our baptism.

Yea, before we come so far, even, at Christ's conceiving, there we hear of Him first, 'Who was conceived by the Holy Ghost'. So, three several times, we there hear of Him. 'Which was conceived by the Holy Ghost'. 'I believe in the Holy Ghost', and 'in the name of the Holy Ghost'. At our baptism, all three. And 'in the mouth of three witnesses is every point sufficiently established'.

St Basil proceeds. 'As from baptism to belief, so from believing to giving glory'. And there, he flatly avoweth – which all the Christian world knew to be true, nor was there ever heretic found so bold as to deny it – that the doxology as they call it, that is, the use of saying, 'Glory be to the Father, the Son and Holy Ghost', this form of concluding Psalms, and hymns, and thanksgivings, was ever received, and retained in the Church from the beginning, as with us still it is. So was baptism, so was thanks for the baptized party, the new member of the Church, so all concluded. So that way we hear of Him there again.

Yet once more, and it is his last. 'As we glorify God, so we bless men; as we give glory to Him, so we receive blessing from Him'. How? The form is often heard, and well known, it is the Apostle's 'The grace of Christ our Lord', 'the love of God' His Father; and 'the fellowship of the Holy Ghost, to be with us'. So after baptism, so after sermon, so is the congregation ever dismissed. Then, there, we glorify Him. And in Him we there are blessed. And so we hear of Him once more, that a Holy Ghost there is.

Upon the matter, no baptism no belief; God no glory, men no blessing, but still we hear of Him. So as if any but see baptism, hear but the creed, be at the daily service, hear the Church rendering glory to God, receiving blessing from the Bishop or Priest; by some of these, or all of these, they cannot choose but hear of the Holy Ghost. There is then no saying for us, 'But we have not so much as heard'. Away with that, and say with St Basil, 'We are baptized in Him; and as we are baptized, so we believe; and as we believe, so glorify we God; and as we glorify God, so bless we men'; bless, and are blessed. These four, they are all here, and they are not far fetched, they have no curious speculation in them, they will serve for any honest or good-hearted Christian to rest in, and they need go no further than, 'In Whom therefore were you baptized?'

Thus we are referred, and we know where we are sure to hear of Him if we stay a little upon 'In Whom baptized', and look better into it, this is not all, but we shall find further, not only that such an one there is, but take more perfect notice of Him. And first, that He is God. And by no other, but by the same steps we went before.

God first. For that we cannot be baptized into any name, but God's alone. The Apostle disputes it at large that it cannot be, that it is not lawful to be baptized into St Peter's name, or into his, or into any name else, but God's only. But in His name we are baptized, even in the name of the Holy Ghost: that proves Him God.

God, secondly. For we believe in Him. We there profess it. Athanasius saith, 'Never any Christian doubted of this, that we believe not in any creature, but in God alone'. Believing then in Him, we acknowledge Him to be God.

God, thirdly. For we ascribe to Him glory. And glory is proper to God only; so proper, that He saith expressly, He will not 'part with it to any other'. But we render Him glory and 'With the Father and the Son, together, He is worshipped and glorified'. Therefore God with them, even in that respect.

Lastly, God, from blessing also, for that is one of God's peculiars. To bless in His name, by putting His name upon children, old and young, upon the congregation, to bless them. But with His name we bless, no less than with the rest. Therefore as they, so He, 'God above all', as to bless, so to be 'blessed for ever'.

And upon these four we rest. These four, To be baptized into Him, To believe in Him, To ascribe glory to Him, To bless by Him, or in His name, they are acts, such acts, as cannot be given to any, but to God only; and so evidently, we there hear of Him, that He is God also. And such are the two acts in the Creed of Constantinople, To be Lord and giver of life, and To speak by the Prophets. Such are many other attributes and works, that cannot agree to any but God, ascribed to the Holy Ghost, which might be and which elsewhere have been alleged. But now we are to keep us to our baptism, and go no further.

And if we will stay yet but a little upon our baptism, and hearken well; as we hear that He is God, so shall we that He is God in unity. For there we hear but 'of one name'. Now as the Apostle reasoneth, 'To Abraham and his seed, were the promises made. He saith not, to the seeds, as of many; but to His Seed, as of one'. So we are baptized, 'not in the names, as of many, but in the name, as of one'. One name and one nature, or essence. 'We are one', saith Christ of two of them; 'They are one', saith St John of all three. This we hear there. *Unum sunt*, but not *unus*. For as from the name we deduce the unity, so from the number, Three, do we the Trinity – one in name and nature, yet distinct between themselves. Distinct in number, as in our baptism; 'The Father, Son, Holy Ghost'. And that number distinct to the sense, as at Christ's baptism; the Father in the voice, the Son in the flood, the Holy Ghost in the shape of a dove. And that showed to be a distinction of persons, in Christ's promise. *Ego*, the person of Christ; *Patrem*, the Person of the Father; and *Paracletum*, the Person of the Holy Ghost. The Holy Ghost, I say, distinct from the Father; 'The Lord and His Spirit hath sent me'. From the Son, 'another Comforter', by 'another' – the Son one, He another. And distinct, as a Person; for to omit other personal acts which properly agree to none but a reasonable nature determined, as to be 'the Lord', to 'speak', 'teach', 'reprove', 'comfort', 'be a witness', to place Bishops, make decrees in council; that which we hear of at our baptism ascribed to Him, to conceive the human nature of Christ, is an act so personal, as in propriety of speech can agree to none, or be affirmed of none, but of an entire person. This we hear.

A Person then, distinct by Himself, yet as a person, not of or for Himself. And this we hear from the very term itself of 'Spirit'. For even as the Son of anyone, so the Spirit of anyone, proceed from him whose Son or Spirit they are. So the Son of God, and Spirit of God, do from God; God of God either. 'In Himself' then, that He is 'the Spirit of the Lord', He proceeds without more ado. Proceeds, and from both. From the Father, the Constantinopolitan Council, for the express words, 'Who proceedeth from the Father'. From the Son, the Council of Toledo, the eight, from the visible sign, where the Son breathed on the Apostles, and willed them from Him to 'receive the Holy Ghost'. And, 'He shall not speak of Himself, but He shall receive of Mine', showeth fully as much. Briefly; sent by the Father, and by the Son too. And so, 'the Spirit of the Father', and 'of the Son' too.

Proceeding from them, and not by way of generation – that is Christ's proper; He is often termed 'the Only begotten', and so none but He – but by way of, 'send forth the Spirit', emission, sending it forth; that is, out of the very body of the word spirit, by spiration, or breathing. One breathing, yet from both; even as the breath, which carrieth the name and resemblance of it, is one yet from both the nostrils, in the body natural.

All these are expressed, or implied, in our baptism. And now lastly, to return home to our purpose, proceeds from them to come to us; is breathed from them, to inspire us; sent by them, to be given us; 'by the Holy Ghost Which is given us' – given to receive, and so to be received of us. Which openeth the way and maketh the passage over to the second question, 'have ye received?' And so, as we see, the two parts follow well and kindly, one upon the other. For this now is the last thing to be heard of Him, that it is not enough to hear of Him, but that we are to receive Him also, and to give account to St Paul that we have so done.

So then, we have now cleared the first question, at our baptism, and have 'heard', That such a one there is; and that He is God; God, in unity of name; Yet in number distinct, and distinct as a Person by Himself; a Person by Himself, yet not of Himself, but proceeding; Proceeding from both Persons, that stand before Him, the Father and the Son; And that breath-wise. And so we have done with that. But yet we have not done though. For the other question must be answered too; no remedy, it imports us. For as good not hear of Him at all, as hear and not receive Him.

Thither then I come. 'Have ye received the Holy Ghost?' Wherein these three points; That we are liable to this question, and to the affirmative part of it, part of it, that we have, and so are bound to receive Him; for so it presupposeth. If we so have, how to know it; If we have not, how to compass it.

How much it importeth us to receive Him, we may esteem by this, that St Paul makes it his first article; begins with it at the first, as the most needful point.

Two things are in it. First, that receive we must. Secondly, of receiving that it must be the Holy Ghost we are to receive.

Receive? What need we receive any spirit, or receive at all? May we not, out of ourselves, work that will serve our turns? No; for holy we must be, if ever we shall rest in His holy Hill, for 'without holiness none shall ever see God'. But holy we cannot be by any habit, moral or acquisite. There is none such in all moral philosophy. As we have our faith by illumination, so have we our holiness by inspiration; receive both, both from without.

To a habit the philosophers came, and so Christians may; but that will not serve, they are to go farther. Our habits acquisite will lift us no farther than they did the heathen men; no farther than the place where they grow, that is, earth and nature. They cannot work beyond their kind – nothing can; nor rise higher than their spring. It is not therefore,

'If you have received the habit', but 'If you have received the Spirit', we must go by.

But then, why 'you have received the Holy Ghost'? No receiving will serve, but of Him? The reason is, it is nothing here below that we seek, but to heaven we aspire. Then, if to heaven we shall, something from heaven must thither exalt us. If 'partakers of the Divine nature' we hope to be, as great and precious promises we have that we shall be, that can be no otherwise than by receiving One in whom the Divine nature is. He being received imparts it to us, and so makes us 'partakers of the divine nature' and that is the Holy Ghost.

For as an absolute necessity there is that we receive the Spirit, else can we not live the life of nature, so no less absolute that we receive the Holy Spirit, else can we not live the life of grace, and so consequently never come to the life of glory.

[. . .]

Look how the breath and the voice in the way of nature go together; even so do the Spirit and the word in the practice of religion. The Holy Ghost is 'Christ's Spirit', and Christ is 'the Word'. And of that Word, 'the word that is preached' to us is an abstract. There must then needs be a nearness and alliance between the one and the other. And indeed, but by our default, 'the word and the Spirit', saith Esay, shall never fail or ever part, but one be received when the other is. We have a plain example of it this day, in St Peter's auditory, and another in Cornelius and his family; even in the sermon-time, 'the Holy Ghost fell upon them' and they so received Him.

Yea, we may see it by this, that in the hearing of the word where He is not received yet He worketh somewhat onward. Upon Felix, took him with a shaking, and further would have gone, but that he put it over to 'a convenient time' which convenient time never came. And upon Agrippa likewise, somewhat it did move him, and more it would, but that he was content to be 'almost a Christian' to take his religion by a little, as it were upon a knife's point, and was afraid to be 'too much' a Christian.

That we see not this effect, that with the word the Spirit is not received as it would be, the reason is it is no sooner gotten than it is lost. We should find this effect, if after we had heard the word, we could get us a little out of the noise about us, and withdraw ourselves some whither, where we might be by ourselves, that when we have heard Him speak to us, we might hear what He would speak in us. When we have heard the voice before us, we might hear the other behind us, 'This is the way'. When the voice that soundeth, the other of Job, 'I heard a voice in silence'– there hear Him reprove, teach, comfort us, within. Upon which texts are grounded the soliloquies, the communing with our own spirit', which are much praised by the ancients, to this purpose; for 'by a little musing or meditation the fire would kindle' and be kept alive, which otherwise will die. And certain it is that many sparks kindled, for want of this, go out again straight, for as fast as it is written in our hearts, it is wiped out again; as fast as the seed is sown, it is picked up by the fowls again, and so our receiving is in vain, the word and the Spirit are severed, which else would keep together.

Lastly, as the word and the Spirit, so the flesh and the Spirit go together. Not all flesh, but this flesh, the flesh that was conceived by the Holy Ghost, this is never without the Holy Ghost by Whom it was conceived; so that, receive one, and receive both. Ever with this blood there runneth still an artery, with plenty of Spirit in it, which maketh that we eat there 'a spiritual meat', and that in that cup we be 'made drink of the Spirit'. There is not only 'putting on of the hands', but after it, 'putting it into our hands'. 'Putting on of hands', in 'receive the bread and the cup'; and 'putting it into our hands', in 'take, eat, drink'. And so, we in case to receive body, blood, Spirit and all, if ourselves be not in fault.

Now then, if we will invite the Spirit indeed, and if each of these, by itself in several, be thus effectual to procure it, put them all, and bind them all together. 'Take to you words', Osee's words, words of earnest invocation. 'Receive' or take to you 'the word', St James' word, 'grafted into you' by the office of preaching. 'Take the holy mysteries of His body and blood'; and the same, the holy arteries of His blessed Spirit. Take all these in one – the attractive of prayer; the word which is 'spirit and life'; the bread of life, and the cup of salvation; and is there not great hope we shall answer St Paul's question as he would have it answered, *affirmative*? 'Have ye received?' Yes; we have received Him. Yes sure. Then, if ever; thus, if by any way. For on earth there is no surer way than to join all these; and He so to be received, if at all.

So, we began with hearing outward, and we end with receiving inward. We began with one Sacrament, Baptism; we end with the other, the Eucharist. We began with that, where we heard of Him; and we end with this other, where we may and shall, I trust, receive Him. And Almighty God grant we so may receive Him at this good time, as in His good time we may be received by Him thither, whence He this day came of purpose to bring us, even to the holy places made without hands, which is His Heavenly kingdom, with God the Father Who prepared it, and God the Son Who purchased it for us!

Whitsun sermon 5, vol. 3, pp. 183–90; 198–200

5

Sacraments

Before James I at Greenwich, Whitsunday, 29 May 1615

The Holy Ghost descended in a bodily shape like a dove upon Him.

Luke 3.22

The great devotion of Andrewes to the work of the Holy Spirit is empha-sized in this discourse on baptism: the descent of the Holy Spirit at the baptism of Christ may be considered greater even than at Pentecost. He affirms baptismal regeneration, a matter of dispute with some Christians then and later: it was prominent in the theology of the Oxford Move-ment.

This is the feast of the Holy Ghost. And here have we the feast in the text, a visible descending of the Holy Ghost.

Another there was, besides this; but this hath the vantage of it, three ways: the worthiness of the Person. Here, it descends upon Christ, Who alone is more worth than all those there. The priority of time: this here was first, and that other, the Holy Ghost but at the second hand. The generality of the good: that other was proper but to one calling, of the Apostles only. All are not Apostles; all are Christians. This of Christ's concerns all Christians; and so the more general by far.

That it is of baptism, is no whit impertinent neither; for this is the feast of baptism. There were 'three thousand' this day baptized by the Apostles, the first Christians that ever were. In memory of that baptism, the Church ever after held a solemn custom of baptizing at this feast. And many, all the year, reserved themselves till then; those except, whom necessity did cause to make more haste.

But, upon the point, both baptisms fell upon this day. That wherewith the Apostles themselves were baptized, of fire. And that wherewith they baptized the people, of water. So that, even this way, it is pertinent also.

To look into the text, there is no man but at the first blush will conceive there is some great matter in hand. First, by the opening of

Heaven; for that opens not for a small purpose. Then, by the solemn presence of so great estates at it; for here is the whole Trinity in person. The Son in the water, the Holy Ghost in the dove, the Father in the voice. This was never so before, but once; never but twice in all the Bible. Once in the Old Testament, and once in the New. In the Old, at the creation, the beginning of Genesis. There find we God, and the Word with God creating, and 'the Spirit of God moving upon the face of the waters'. And now here again, at Christ's christening in the New.

The faces of the Cherubims are one toward the other; that is there is a mutual correspondence between these two. That was at the creation; this, a creation too: 'if any be in Christ, he is a new creature' of this new creation. That was the genesis, that is, 'the generation' of the world; this, 'the regeneration', or spiritual new birth, whereby we be born again the sons of God. And better not born at all, than not so born again.

This then, being every way as great, (indeed, the greater of the twain) meet it were, they all should present themselves at this, no less than at that; and every one have his part in it, as we see they have. All, I say, seeing the commission for baptism was to run in all their names, and itself ever to be ministered accordingly.

To lay forth the members of the division. A double baptism we have here; double for the parties, and double for the parts.

For the parties; we have here two parties. First the people. Then Christ.

For the parts; we have here two parts. For this first, both of Christ and the people, was but John's baptism, was but, as they call it, 'water-baptism.' But there is another part besides to be had, even 'the baptism of the Holy Ghost'.

That second part is set down in a sequel of four:

For first, after John's baptism, Christ prays. Then, after His prayer, Heaven opens. After Heaven open, the Holy Ghost descends. Lastly, after His descent, comes the voice. And these four make up the other part, and both together a full baptism.

Of these then in order. Of the people's baptism. Of Christ's baptism. Christ's by water, and then by the Holy Ghost. In which, the four: Christ's prayer, Heaven open, the Dove, and the voice.

'It came to pass, that when', etc. Two baptisms we have here: the people's first. Then Christ's. How it should come to pass the people should be baptized, we see good reason; but not how it should come to pass that Christ also. The people, they came 'confessing their sins', and so needed 'the baptism of repentance' – so was John's baptism. For they were not 'baptized', but, to use the Apostle's word, 'even soused over head and ears in their sins', in 'many foolish and noisome lusts, which drown men in perdition', they had need to be washed from the wallow of their sin they had long lain in.

Whitsun sermon 8, vol. 3, pp. 241–3

Before James I at Whitehall, Christmas Day, 1623

That in the dispensation of the fullness of times, He might gather together in one all things in Christ, both which are in Heaven, and which are on earth, even in Him.

Ephesians 1.10

At the end of a Nativity sermon, Andrewes affirms that the feast should be honoured with the proper devotion of the Eucharist and declares the nature and unique quality of the sacrament, affirming the Real Presence but refusing the doctrine of Transubstantiation. Eutyches in the fourth century AD denied that the humanity of Christ was of the same substance as ours, and taught that there was only one nature in his incarnate person.

We shall better dispense the season, if we gather to prayers, to God's word; if we begin with them, if with the dispensation of His holy mysteries gather to that specially.

For there we do not gather to Christ or of Christ, but we gather Christ Himself; and gathering Him we shall gather the tree and fruit and all upon it. For as there is a recapitulation of all in Heaven and earth in Christ, so there is a recapitulation of all in Christ in the holy Sacrament. You may see it clearly: there is in Christ the Word eternal for things in Heaven; there is also flesh for things on earth. Semblably; the Sacrament consisteth of a Heavenly and of a terrene part, (it is Irenaeus' own words); the Heavenly – there the word too – the abstract of the other; the earthly – the element.

And in the elements, you may observe, there is a fullness of the seasons of the natural year; of the corn flour or harvest in the one; bread; of the winepress or vintage in the other, wine. And in the Heavenly, of the 'wheat-corn', whereto He compareth Himself – bread, even 'the living Bread' (or, 'Bread of life') 'that came down from Heaven'; the true Manna, whereof we may gather each his gomer. And again, of Him, the true Vine as He calls Himself – the blood of the grapes of that Vine. Both these issuing out of this day's recapitulation, both in 'Thou hast prepared a body for Me' of this day.

And the gathering or vintage of these two in the blessed Eucharist, is as I may say a kind of hypostatical union of the sign and the thing signified, so united together as are the two natures of Christ. And even from this Sacramental union do the Fathers borrow their resemblance, to illustrate by it the personal union in Christ; I name Theodoret for the Greek, and Gelasius for the Latin Church, that insist upon it both, and press it against Eutyches. That even as in the Eucharist neither part is evacuate or, turned into the other, but abides still in his former nature and substance, no more is either of Christ's natures annulled, or one of them converted into the other, as Eutyches held, but each nature remaineth still full and whole in his own kind. And backwards; as the two natures in Christ, so the sign and the thing signified in the Sacrament. And this latter device, of the substance of the bread: and wine to be flown away and gone, and in the room of it a remainder of nothing else but accidents to stay behind, was to them not known, and had it been true, had made for Eutyches and against them. And this for the likeness of union in both.

Now for the word 'gathering together in one'. It is well known the holy Eucharist itself is called *Synaxis*, by no name more usual in all antiquity that is a 'collection or gathering'. For so it is in itself; for at the celebration of it, though we gather to prayer and to preaching, yet that is the principal gathering the Church hath, which is itself called a 'collection' too by the same name from the chief; for 'where the body is there the eagles will be gathered', and so one *Synaxis* begets another.

And last, there is a 'dispensation' – that word in it too, that most clearly. For it is our office, we are styled by the Apostle 'dispensers of the mysteries of God'; and in and by them, of all the benefits that came to mankind by this dispensation in the fullness of season of all that are recapitulate, in Christ.

Which benefits are too many to deal with. One shall serve as the sum of all that the very end of the Sacrament is to gather again to God and His favour, if it happen, as oft it doth, we scatter and stray from Him. And to gather us as close and near as food for nourishment, that is as near as near may be.

And as to gather us to God, so likewise each to other mutually; expressed lively in the symbols of many grains into the one, and many grapes into the other. The Apostle is plain that we are all 'one bread and one body, so many as are partakers of one bread', so moulding us as it were into one loaf altogether. The gathering to God refers still to things in Heaven, this other, to men to the things in earth here. All under one head, by the common faith; all into one body mystical by mutual charity. So shall we well enter into the dispensing of this season, to begin with.

And even thus to be recollected at this feast by the Holy Communion into that blessed union, is the highest perfection we can in this life aspire unto. We then are at the highest pitch, at the very best we shall ever attain to on earth, what time we newly come from it; gathered to Christ, and by Christ to God; stated in all whatsoever He hath gathered and laid up against His next coming. With which gathering here in this world we must content and stay ourselves, and wait for the consummation of all at His coming again. For there is a 'behold I come' yet to come.

This gathering thus here begun, it is to take end, and, to have the full accomplishment at the last and great gathering of all, which shall be of the quick and of the dead, When He shall 'send His Angels, and they shall gather His elect from the corners of the earth', shall 'gather the wheat into the barn, and the tares to the fire'. And then, and never till then, shall be the fullness indeed, when God shall be not, as now He is, somewhat in everyone, but 'all in all'; 'and there shall be neither time' nor season 'any more'. No fullness then but the fullness of eternity, and in it the fullness of all joy. To which, in the several seasons of our being 'gathered to our fathers', He vouchsafe to bring us; that as the year, so the fullness of our lives may end in a Christmas, a merry joyful feast, as that is!

Nativity sermon 16, vol. 1, pp. 281–3

Before James I at Whitehall, Easter Day, 13 April 1623

Wherefore art Thou red in Thine apparel, and Thy garments like him that treadeth in the winefat?

Isaiah 53.1–3

A rather Metaphysical reflection on colour symbolism leads to an explication of both Word and Eucharist as essential in worship.

You see how Christ's garments came to be 'red.' Of the winepress that made them so we have spoken, but not the colour itself. A word of that too. It was His colour at His Passion. They put Him in purple; then it was His weed in derision, and so was it in earnest. Both 'red' it was itself, and so He made it more with the dye of His own blood. And the same colour He is now in again at His rising. Not with His own now, but with the blood of the wounded Edomites, whom treading under His feet, their blood bestained Him and His apparel. So one and the same colour at both; dying and rising in red; but with difference as much as is between His own and His enemies' blood.

The spouse in the Canticles asked of her Beloved's colours saith of Him, 'My Beloved is white and red'. 'White' of His own proper: so He was when He showed Himself in kind, 'transfigured' in the Mount; His apparel then so 'white', no 'fuller in the earth could come near it'. 'White' of Himself; how comes He 'red' then? Not of Himself that, but for us. That is our natural colour, we are born 'polluted in our own blood'. It is sin's colour that, for shame is the colour of sin. Our sins saith Esay 'are as crimson, of as deep dye as any purple'. This, the true tincture of our sins, the Edomites' colour right, for Edom is red. The tincture I say, first of our sin original, dyed in the wool; and then again of our sins actual, dyed in the cloth too. Twice dyed; so was Christ twice. Once in His own, again in His enemies', right 'twice dyed', a perfect full colour, a true purple, of a double dye His too. So was it meet for crimson sinners to have a crimson Saviour; a Saviour of such a colour it behoved us to have. Coming then to save us, off went His white, on went our red; laid by His own righteousness to be clothed with our sin. He to wear our colours, that we His; He in our red, that we in His white. So we find our 'robes' are not only 'washed clean', but dyed a pure white in the blood of the Lamb. Yea, He died and rose again both in our colours, that we might die and rise too in His. We fall now again upon the same point in the colours we did before in the cups. He to drink the sour vinegar of our wild grapes, that we might drink His sweet in the cup of blessing. O cup of blessing, may we say of this cup! O beautiful garment of that colour! 'Glorious to Him, no less fruitful to us'. He in Mount Golgotha like to us, that we in Mount Tabor like to Him. This is the substance of our rejoicing in this colour.

One more; how well this colour fits Him in respect of His two titles, 'speaking in righteousness', and 'mighty to save'. 'Speaking in right-eousness', is to wear red; 'mighty to save' is so too. The first. To whom is this colour given? Scarlet is allowed the degree of Doctors. Why? for their speaking righteousness to us, the righteousness of God, that which Christ spake. Nay, even they which speak but the righteousness of man's law, they are honoured with it too. But Christ 'spake so as never man spake' and so call ye none on earth Doctor but One; none in comparison of Him. So of all, He to wear it. This ye shall observe in the

Revelation; at the first appearing of the Lamb, there was a book with seven seals. No man would meddle with it; the Lamb took it, opened the seals, read it, read out of it a lecture of righteousness to the whole world; the righteousness of God, that shall make us so before Him. Let Him be arrayed in scarlet; it is His due, His Doctor's weed.

This is no new thing. The heathen king propounded it for a reward to any that could read the hand-writing on the wall. Daniel did it, and had it. 'But behold, a greater than Daniel is here. Thus was it in the Law. This colour was the ground of the Ephod, a principal ingredient into the Priest's vesture. Why? For, 'his lips were to preserve knowledge', all to require the law from his mouth. And indeed, the very lips themselves that we speak righteousness with, are of the same colour. In the Canticles it is said, 'His lips are like a scarlet thread'. And the fruit of the lips hath God created peace, and the fruit of peace is sown in righteousness; and till that be sown and spoken, never any hope of true peace.

Enough for speaking. What say you to the other, 'mighty to save', which of the twain seems the more proper to this time and place? I say that way it fits Him too, this colour. Men of war, great captains, 'mighty to save' us from the enemies, they take it to themselves, and their colour it is of right A plain text for it, Nahum the second. 'Their valiant men', or captains, 'are in scarlet'. And I told you Christ by Daniel is called 'Captain Messias', and so well might. So in His late conflict with Edom He showed Himself, fought for us even to blood. Many a bloody wound it cost Him, but returned with the spoil of His enemies, stained with their blood; and whoso is able so to do, is worthy to wear it. So in this respect also, so in both; His colours become Him well.

Shall I put you in mind, that there is in these two, in either of them, a kind of winepress? In 'mighty to save', it is evident; trodden in one press, treading in another. Not so evident in 'the speaking of righteousness'. Yet even in that also, there is a press going. For when we read, what do we but gather grapes here and there; and when we study what we have gathered, then are we even 'in the winepress', and press them we do, and press out of them that which daily you taste of. I know there is great odds in the liquors so pressed, and that 'a cluster of Ephraim is worth a whole vintage of Abiezer'; but for that, every man as he may. Nay, it may be further said, and that truly, that even this great title, 'Mighty to save', comes under 'speaking in righteousness'. There is in the word of righteousness a saving power. 'Take the word', saith St James, 'graft it in you, it is able to save your souls'; even that wherein we of this calling in a sort participate with Christ, while 'by attending to reading and doctrine we save both ourselves and them that hear us'; we tread down sin, and save sinners from 'seeking death in the error of their life'.

But though there be in the word a saving power, yet is not a saving power in that, nor in that only; there is no press beside. For this press is going continually among us, but there is another that goes but at times. But in that, it goes at such times as it falls in fit with the winepress here. Nay, falls in most fit of all the rest. For of it comes very wine indeed, the blood of the grapes of the true Vine, which in the blessed Sacrament is reached to us, and with it is given us that for which it was given, even remission of sins. Not only represented therein, but even exhibited to us. Both which when we partake, then have we a full and perfect communion with Christ this day; of His speaking righteousness in the word preached, of His power to save in the holy Eucharist ministered. Both presses run for us, and we to partake them both.

Resurrection sermon 17, vol. 3, pp. 75–8

Before James I at Whitehall, 5 November 1617

That we being delivered out of the hand of our enemies might serve Him without fear, In holiness and righteousness before Him, all the days of our life.

Luke 1.74–5

After the customary discourse on deliverance from the Gunpowder Plot, Andrewes speaks of holiness, and then moves to reverence in worship. The sermon in the previous extract stresses the importance of both Word and Sacrament; here he deplores setting any privileging of the sermon above the sacrament.

Thus serve we Him in His holy worship: how serve we Him in His Holy things? How serve we Him in our 'holiness' there? I will begin, and take up the same complaint that the Prophet Malachi doth. For 'The table of the Lord is not regarded'. That Sacrament that ever hath been counted of all holies the most holy, the highest and most solemn service of God, where are delivered to us the holy symbols, the precious memorials of our greatest delivery of all; why of all others they speed worst. How are they in many places denied any reverence at all, even that which prayer, which other parts have? No service then, no servants there; but bidden guests, hail fellows, homely and familiar, as one neighbour with another. And not only 'in practice' none they have, but 'in theory' it is holden none they ought to have. And that so holden as rather than they shall have any, some will suffer for it or rather for their own proud folly in refusing it. What time they 'take the cup of salvation', they will not invoke, at least not be 'in the type of invocation'; as the King, the Prophet, would. What time they receive 'the cup of blessing' they will not receive it as a blessing, as children receive it from their parents, and their children from them. Both which, invocation and receiving a blessing, were never done but 'on their knees'. What shall the rest look for, if thus we serve Him when we are at the holiest?

Shall we now come to the service indeed? 'Service' the word here in my text. It is no new thing for one 'type' to carry away the name of the 'class' from the rest, as in this; for though there be other parts of God's service, yet prayer hath borne away the name of service from them all. The Hebrews call their Common Prayer 'service'. And the Greeks their 'liturgy', and that is so too. And we, when we say, At Service time, and the Service book, and refuse to be present at divine service, mean so likewise. And God Himself seems to go before us, and direct us so to do; for His house he hath named 'the house of prayer', observing the rule, to give it the denomination from that which is the chiefest service in it. As indeed when all is done, devotion is the proper and most kindly work of 'holiness'; and in that serve we God, if ever we serve Him. Now, in what honour this part of 'holiness' is; what account we make of this service, do but tell the number of them that be here at it, and ye shall need no other certificate that in His service we serve Him but slenderly.

'Thou hast magnified Thy Name and Thy word above all things', saith the Psalm. After invocation then of His Name, let us see how we serve His word, that part of His service which in this age – I might say in the error of this age – carries away all. For what is it to 'serve God in holiness'? Why, to go to a sermon; all our holiday 'holiness'; yea and our working-day too, both are come to this, to hear – nay, I dare not say that, I cannot prove it – but to be at a sermon.

The word is holy, I know, and I wish it all the honour that may be; but God forbid we should think that 'everything is in this one thing'. All our 'holiness' is in hearing, all our service ear-service; that were in effect as much as to say all the body were an ear. An error it is to shut up His service into any one part, which is diffused through all, another, so to do into this one. It is well known that all the time of the Primitive Church, the sermon was ever done before the service begun. And that to the sermon, heathen men, infidels, and Jews, heretics, schismatics, 'possessed', 'catechumens', 'penitents', 'ready for baptism', 'new hearers', all these, all sorts of people were admitted; but when they went to service, when the liturgy began, all these were voided, not one of them suffered to stay. It were strange that that should be the only or the chief service of God, whereat they which were held no servants of God, no part of the Church, might and did remain no less freely than they that were.

But even this holy word, wherein all our 'holiness' is, how serve ye Him in it? Nay we serve Him not, we take the greatest liberty there of all other. We come to it if we will, we go our ways when we will, stay no longer than we will, and listen to it while we will; and sleep out, or turn us and talk out or sit still and let our minds rove the rest whither they will; take stitch at a phrase or word, and censure it how we will. So the word serves us to make us sport; we serve not it. At this part of our service in 'holiness', we demean ourselves with such liberty – nay licentiousness rather, that holy it may be, but sure service it is not, nothing like. And truly it is a notable stratagem of Satan to shrink up all our 'holiness' into one part, and into that one where we may be or not be; being, hear or not hear; hearing, mind or not mind; minding, either remember or forget; give no account to any what we do or not do; only stay out the hour, if that, and then go our way, many of us as wise as we came; but all in a manner hearing, as Ezekiel complaineth, a sermon preached no otherwise than we do a ballad sung; and do even no more of the one than we do of the other. Eye-service God liketh not, I am sure, no more should I think doth He ear-service. 'Speak on, Lord, for Thy servant heareth', and well if that but scarce that otherwhile; but 'Speak on, Lord', whether Thy servant hear or no – would any of us be content with such service? Yet this is all, to this it is come. Thus we 'serve Him in holiness', this service must serve Him, as the world goes; for if this way we serve Him not, we serve Him not at all.

Gunpowder Treason sermon 9, vol. 4, pp. 375–8

Before James I at Whitehall, Whitsunday, 4 June 1620

This is He that came by water and blood, even Jesus Christ; not by water only, but by water and blood.

1 John 5.6

Coming to the end of a Whitsunday sermon, Andrewes makes an application of the water and the blood in baptism and Eucharist, and urges worthy preparation for communion, having a comment also on profane swearing.

The Apostle saith, 'the Spirit speaks evidently'; that is, his noise and speech is evidently to be distinguished from those of other spirits. His coming in tongues this day, showeth no less. Which sign of speech doth best and most properly sort there, with a witness. For a witness, what he hath to testify, speaks it out vocally.

What noise then is heard from us? (What breathe we? What 'speaks the Spirit manifestly' from our mouths?) if cursing and bitterness, and many a foul oath, if this noise be heard from us; if we 'bluster out threatening and slaying'– that noise; if 'rotten, corrupt, obscene communication' come out of our mouths? We are of Galilee, and our very speech 'bewrayeth' us. This is not the breath of the Spirit, this He speaks not; evidently He speaks it not. It is not the tongue of Heaven this: not 'as the Spirit gave them utterance', no utterance of the Spirit's giving. Some of Christ's water would do well to wash these out of our mouths. The speech sounding of the Spirit, is a sign of the true Spirit.

The last, but the surest of all, 'all these things the Spirit works'. And the work is as clearly to be distinguished as the speech. Each spirit hath his proper work, and is known by it. No man ever saw the works of the devil come from the Spirit of God. Be not deceived, the works of uncleanness come from no spirit, but 'the unclean spirit'. The works of Cain from 'the spirit of envy'; the works of Demas from 'the spirit of the world'. All the gross errors of our life from the spirit of error. But this, this is 'the Spirit of truth'; and the breath, the speech, the operations of Him, bear witness that He is so. Now, if He will depose that 'the water and blood' Christ came in, He came in for us, and we our parts in them; in them, and in them both; and so deposing, if we feel His breath, hear His speech, see His works according, we may receive His 'witness' then, for His 'witness' is true.

Now, that upon this day, the day of the Spirit, 'the Spirit' may come and bear this 'witness' to Christ's 'water and blood', there is to be water and blood for 'the Spirit' to bear witness to. So was there ever as this day, in the Church of Christ, the 'three thousand', this day baptized by St Peter. And 'blood': never a more frequent Eucharist than at Pentecost, in honour of this Spirit, to which St Paul made such haste with his alms and offerings. Witness the great works done by Pentecostal oblations; which very oblations remain in some Churches to this day.

So are we now come to the reversal, to the last 'not only'; and here it is. Not in the Spirit alone, but 'in water and blood'. As not these without the Spirit, so neither the Spirit without these, that is, without the Sacrament wherein these be. So have we a perfect circle now. Neither 'in water' without 'blood', nor in 'blood' without 'water'; nor in them alone without 'the Spirit'; nor in the Spirit alone, without them.

This day Christ comes to us 'in blood', in the Sacrament of it so. But as we said before, either is in other. 'Blood' is not ministered, but there is an ingredient of the purifying virtue of 'water' withal in it: so He comes in 'water' too. Yea, comes in 'water' first so lie they in the text; 'water' to go before with us. So did it, at the very institution itself of this Sacrament. The 'pitcher of water', and he that carried it, was not in vain given for a sign; went not before them that were sent to make ready for it, for nothing.

It had a meaning, that water, and it had a use. Their feet were washed with it, and their feet being clean, they were 'clean every whit'. Many make ready for it, that see neither water nor pitcher. It were well they did, their feet would be washed; so would their hands 'in innocency', that are to go to His altar. 'In innocency', that is, in a steadfast purpose of keeping ourselves clean: so to come. For to come and not with that purpose, better not come at all. To find a feeling of this purpose before, and to mark well the success and effect that doth follow after. For if it fail us continually, Christ did not come. For when He comes, though it be in 'blood', yet He comes with 'water' at the same time. Ever in both, never in one alone.

His blood is not only drink to nourish, but medicine to purge. To nourish the new man, which is faint and weak, God wot; but to take down the old, which is rank in most. It is the proper effect of His blood; it doth 'cleanse our consciences from dead works, to serve the living God'.

Which if we find it doth, Christ is come to us, as He is to come. And the Spirit is come, and puts His test. And if we have this test, we may go our way in peace; we have kept a right feast to him, and to the memory of His coming.

Whitsun sermon 13, vol. 3, pp. 357–9

6

Preaching

Before James I at Greenwich, Whitsunday, 24 May 1618

And it shall come to pass in the last days, saith God, I will pour out of My Spirit upon all flesh: and your sons and your daughters shall prophesy, and your young men shall see visions, and your old men shall dream dreams.

Acts 2.16–21, referring to Joel

Andrewes naturally had strong views about preaching. As has been seen, he condemned the exaltation of the sermon above the sacrament (p. 60). He was also, like other orthodox churchmen of the time, opposed to unlicensed 'prophesying' of the kind conducted by some of the Puritans. His objections are worth quoting at some length, because the issue was a major source of controversy in his time and in the decades that followed. Here he warns of the consequences of ignoring biblical prophecies of the Last Day and makes reference to 'Holland' – the Dutch Calvinists. 'They shall prophesy' must be reinforced by 'whosoever shall call upon the name of the Lord'. He plays on the Latin gratia *and* gratum *– grace and thanks.*

But what say you to 'visions' and 'dreams' here? Little; they pertain not to us. The text saith it not. You remember the two pourings. One upon their 'sons'. The other upon His 'servants'. This latter is it by which we come in. We are not of their 'sons', we claim not by that; God made us His 'servants', for by that word we hold.

Now in this latter pouring on His 'servants', which only concerns us, 'visions' and 'dreams' are left out quite. If any pretend them now, we say with Jeremiah, 'Let a dream go for a dream', and 'Let My word', saith the Lord, 'be spoken as My word': 'What, mingle you chaff and wheat?' We are to lay no point of religion upon them now; prophecy, preaching is it, we to hold ourselves unto now. As for 'visions' and 'dreams', 'let them go'.

But then, for prophecy in this sense of opening or interpreting Scriptures, is the Spirit poured upon all flesh so? Is this of Joel a proclamation for liberty of preaching, that all, young and old, men-servants and maid-servants may fall to it? Nay, the she sex, St Paul took order for that betimes, cut them off with his 'I do not wish women [to speak in the church]'. But what for the rest? may they? For to this sense hath this Scripture been wrested by the enthusiasts of former ages, and still is, by the Anabaptists now. And by mistaking of it, way given to a foul error, as if all were let loose, all might claim and take upon them, forsooth, to prophesy.

Nothing else this but a malicious device of the devil, to pour contempt upon this gift. For, indeed, bring it to this once, and what was this day falsely surmised will then be justly affirmed 'full of new wine', or 'with a vacant mind', whether you will: but 'drunken' Prophets then indeed; howbeit 'not with wine' as Esay saith, but with another as heady a humour, and that doth intoxicate the brain as much as any must or new wine; even of self-conceited ignorance, whereof the world grows too full. But it was no part of Joel's meaning, nor St Peter's neither, to give way to this phrensy.

No? Is it not plain? The Spirit is poured 'upon all flesh'. True, but not upon all to prophesy though. The text warrants no such thing. In the one place it is, 'And your sons shall': in the other, 'and my servants shall'. But neither is it, All their 'sons'; nor, All His 'servants' shall. Neither, indeed, can it be. There must be some 'sons', and some 'servants', to prophesy to, to whom these Prophets may be sent, to whom this prophecy may come. 'All flesh' may not be cut out into tongues; some left for ears, some auditors needs. Else a Cyclopian Church will grow upon us, where all were speakers, nobody heard another.

How then, shall the Spirit be poured 'upon all flesh'? Well enough. The Spirit of Prophecy is not all God's Spirit, He hath more beside. If the spirit or grace of prophecy upon some, 'the spirit of grace and prayer', in Zachary, upon the rest. So between them both, the Spirit will be 'upon all flesh', and the proposition hold true: 'they shall prophesy' must not make us forget '[whosoever] shall call [upon the name of the Lord]'. All the Spirit goes not away in prophesying, some left for that too; and there is the 'whosoever shall call' and no where else.

But if St Peter will not serve, St Paul shall; he is plain. 'Ye may all prophesy one by one': what, the skippers of Holland and all I trow not. But 'all' there, is plain. 'All', that is, 'all' that be 'Prophets'. And I wish with all my heart, as did Moses, that 'all God's people were Prophets'; but, till they be so, I wish they may not prophesy: no more would Moses neither. Now in the same Epistle, St Paul holds it for a great absurdity, to hold 'all' are Prophets. With a kind of indignation he asks it, 'What, are all Prophets?' No more than 'all Apostles' – as much the one as the other. Then, if 'all' be not 'Prophets', all may not prophesy, sure. For, with the Apostle in the same place, 'the operation', that is, the act of prophesying, 'the administration', that is, the office or calling, and 'the grace', that is, the enabling gift, these three are ever to go together. No act in the Church lawfully done, without them all. Then the Apostle's 'You all may' is, All you may that have the gift.

And not you that have it neither, 'the gift', unless you have the calling too; for as God sent gifts, so He gave men also, 'some Apostles, some Prophets'. Men for gifts, as well as 'gifts for men'. 'He sent' in Christ as well as 'He anointed', last year. And in His servants, 'He called' as well as 'gave talents'. Not to be parted, these.

I conclude then. 'And they shall prophesy'; but such as have been at the door of the Tabernacle, as have been the sons of the Prophets, men set apart for that end. And yet even they also, so as they take not themselves at liberty to prophesy whatsoever takes them in the tongue, the dreams of their own heads, or the visions of their own hearts; but remember their 'above' and know there be Spirits also to whom 'their spirits be subject'. So much for the seventeenth and eighteenth verses.

But how now come we thus suddenly to the signs of the latter day, and to the day itself? For they follow close, you see. It is somewhat strange that from 'and they shall prophesy' He is straight at doomsday without more ado.

The reasons which I find the Fathers render of it are these:

First, the close joining of them is to meet with another dream that hath troubled the Church much. And that is, that it may be there will be another pouring yet after this, and more Prophets rise still. Every other-while, some such upstart spirits there are, would fain make us so believe. Here is a discharge for them.

No, saith Joel, look for no more such days as this after this. Therefore to this day he joins immediately, from this day He goes presently to the latter day, as if He said, You have all you shall have. When this pouring hath run so far as it will, then cometh the end; when this is done, the world is done; no new spirit, no new effusion, this is the last. From Christ's departure till His return again; from this day of Pentecost, a 'great day and a notable', till the last 'great and notable day' of all; between these two days, no more such day. Therefore, in the beginning of the text, He called them 'the last days', because no days to come after them. No pouring to be looked for from this first day of those last: No

other but this, till 'the very last day of all'; till He pour down fire to con-
sume 'all flesh' that, by the fire this day kindled by these fiery tongues,
shall not be brought to know Him, and call upon His name.

A second is, being to speak by and by of 'shall be saved', that we
should be saved, He would let us see what it is we should be saved from.
That helpeth much to make us esteem of our saving. Saved then
from what? 'from blood, and fire, and the smoulder of smoke'; that is,
from the heavy signs here, and from that which is after these, and
beyond all these far, 'the great and terrible day of the Lord'. This sight
of 'from whence,' will make us apprize our saving at a higher rate and
think it worth our care then, in that day to be saved.

And last, it is set here, 'to quicken us,' 'so that knowing this terror',
saith St Paul, that entering into a sad and sober consideration of it, and
'the terror' of it, we might stir up ourselves by it, to prepare for it. And
set it is between both, to dispose us the better to both. To that which is
past, 'and they shall prophesy', to awake our attention to that; and to
that which follows, '[whosoever] shall call' to kindle our devotion in
that, and so by both to make sure our salvation.

'The day of the Lord', the Prophet calls it; as it were opposing it to 'the
day of the servant', to our days here. As if he said, These are your days,
and you use them indeed, as if they were your own. You pour out yourselves into all riot, and know no other pouring out but that; you see not
any great use of prophesying, think it might well enough be spared; you
speak your pleasures of it and say, 'full of new wine', or to like effect,
when you list. These are your days. But know this, when yours are done,
God hath His day too, and His day will come at last, and it will come
terribly when it comes.

When that day comes, how then? the Prophet's ordinary question,
'What will ye do at the last?' how will you be saved, in 'in that day?' [. . .]

Two errors there be, and I wish them reformed: one, as if prophesying
were all we had to do, we might dispense with invocation, let it go, leave
it to the choir. That is an error. Prophesying is not all, 'shall call upon'
is to come in too; we to join them, and jointly to observe them, to make
a conscience of both. It is the oratory of prayer poured out of our hearts
shall save us, no less than the oratory of preaching poured in at our ears.

The other is, of them that do not wholly reject it, yet so depress it, as
if in comparison of prophesying it were little worth. Yet, we see, by the
frame of this text, it is the higher end; the calling on us by prophecy, is
but that we should call on the Name of the Lord. All prophesying, all
preaching, is but to this end. And indeed prophecy is but 'grace freely
given'; and ever 'freely given' is for 'giving thanks', a part and a special

part whereof is invocation. There is then, as a conscience to be made of both, so a like conscience to be made of both; not to set up the one and magnify it, and to turn our back on the other and vilify it. For howsoever we give good words of invocation, yet what our conceit is our deeds show.

I love not to dash one religious duty against another, or, as it were, to send challenges between them. But as much as the text saith, so much may I say; and that is, that it hath three special prerogatives, by this verse of the Prophet.

First, it is 'I will pour out', ours, properly; and 'I will pour out My Spirit' the pouring out of our spirit, to answer that of God's Spirit in the text. 'They shall prophesy' is not ours, none of our act, but the act of another. The stream of our times tends all to this. To make religion nothing but an auricular profession, a matter of ease, a mere sedentary thing, and ourselves merely passive in it; sit still, and hear a Sermon and two Anthems, and be saved; as if by the act of the choir, or of the preacher, we should so be, (for these be their acts) and we do nothing ourselves, but sit and suffer; without so much as any thing done by us, any 'I will pour out' on our parts at all; not so much as this, of calling on the Name of the Lord.

The second: this hath the 'whosoever'. We would fain have it, 'Whosoever heard the prophet', he that hears so many sermons a week cannot choose but be saved; but it will not be. No; here stand we preaching, and hearing sermons; and neither they that hear prophesying, nay nor they that prophesy themselves, can make a 'whosoever' of either. Witness 'Lord, we have prophesied in Thy name', and, 'Lord thou hast preached in our streets', and yet it would do them no good; 'I do not know you' was their answer for all that.

And yet how fain would some be a prophesying! It would not save them, though they were; and is it not a preposterous desire? We love to meddle with that pertains not to us, and will do us no good: that which is our duty and would do us good, that care we not for.

Tongues were given for prophecy. True; but no 'whosoever' there, for all that; but to whom none are given to prophesy, to them yet are there given to invocate. And there comes it in, the 'whosoever' lies there. 'My Spirit on all flesh' – here it comes in; at invocation, not at the other. Let it suffice; it is not 'whosoever shall prophesy' here, 'whosoever shall call upon' it is. The Prophet saith it, the Apostles say it both. Peter here; Paul, Romans, tenth chapter, and thirteenth verse.

Last, this is sure, 'shall call upon' stands nearest, it joins closest to 'shall be saved'. Both one breath, one sentence; the words touch, there is nothing between them. 'Shall be saved' is not joined hard to 'they shall prophesy', it is removed farther off. To 'shall call upon' it is a degree nearer at least. Nay the very next of all.

The text shows this, in a sort, but the thing itself more; for when all comes to all, when we are even at last cast, 'shall be saved' or 'no shall be saved', then, as if there were some special virtue in 'shall call upon', we are called upon to use a few words or signs to this end, and so sent out of the world with 'shall call upon' in our mouths. Dying, we call upon men for it; living, we suffer them to neglect it. It was not for nothing it stands so close, it even touches salvation; it is, we see, the very immediate act next before it.

And yet I would not leave you in any error concerning it. To end this point; shall 'shall call upon' serve then? needs there nothing but it? no faith, no life? St Paul answers this home; he is direct, Romans the tenth; 'How can they call upon Him, unless they believe?' So invocation presupposeth faith. And as peremptory he is, 'Let everyone that calleth on', nay, that but 'nameth the Name of the Lord, depart from iniquity': so it presupposeth life too. For 'if we incline to wickedness in our hearts, God will not hear us'. No invocation that, not truly so called; a provocation rather. But put these two, faith and 'turn away from iniquity' to it, and so whoso calleth upon Him, I will put him in good sureties, one Prophet and two Apostles, both to assure him he shall be saved.

And that is it we all desire, to be 'saved'. 'Saved' indefinitely. Apply it to any dangers, not in the day of the Lord only, but even in this our day; for some terrible days we have even here. I will tell you of one; the signs here set down bring it to my mind. A day we were saved from, the day of the Powder-treason, which may seem here in a sort to be described – 'blood and fire, and the vapour of smoke'; a 'terrible' day sure, but nothing to 'the Day of the Lord'.

From that we were saved; but we all stand in danger, we all need saving, from this. When this day comes, another manner of fire, another manner of smoke. That fire never burnt, that smoke never rose; but this 'fire' shall burn and never be 'quenched', this 'smoke' shall not vanish, but 'ascend for ever'. I say no more, but in that, in this, in all, 'Whosoever shall call, shall be saved'; invocation rightly used is the way to be safe.

Whitsun sermon 11, vol. 3, pp. 313–6, 318–21

His own rule for preaching is expressed through injunction and prayer

Before Preaching

Let the preacher labour to be heard gladly, intelligently, obediently. And let him not question that he can do better by the piety of his prayers than by the fluency of his speech. By praying for himself and for them he is going to address, let him be a bedesman or ever he be a teacher: and approaching devoutly, before he put forth a speaking tongue, let him lift up to God a thirsty soul, that so he may give out what from Him he hath drunk in, and empty out what he hath first replenished.

Therefore of our very Lord and Master I cease not to ask that, whether by the utterances of his Scriptures or by the converse of brethren or by the inward and sweeter teaching of his inspiration, He will vouchsafe to learn me what things I can in such sort put forth and in such sort assert, that in my statements and assertions I may alway tarry fast in the Truth. Of this very Truth itself I ask to be taught the many more things I wot not of, of whom I have gotten the small store I wot of.

Preces Privatae, p. 257

7

Scripture

Before James I at Whitehall, 5 November 1609

But He turned, and rebuked them, and said, Ye know not what manner of spirit ye are of.

Luke 9.54–6 [James and John wanted to call down fire upon the inhospitable Samaritans]

The prayers and preaching of Andrewes were deeply rooted in Scripture. He was concerned that the Bible should be widely known, but that it should be read and interpreted with caution, and not used to support any private fancy. In this sermon he stresses the importance of knowledge to support and regulate faith, making much of the Latin word nescitis *– 'ye know not'. He warns against Christians depending too much on the Old Testament, as the Puritans were often accused of doing.*

It would strike such a fear – the burning of the town – into all the towns about, that Christ should never after want receiving; and it would salve Christ's reputation much, who had been thought too great a favourer of these Samaritans.

But Christ never stands weighing these, but for all the parties were Samaritans, parties not to be favoured; for all it is made His quarrel, not He; for all their means should be by miracle, which cannot be misliked; for all this, turns and rebukes them. Never thinks the motion worth the answering, as being evil 'of its own nature', but rebukes them for moving it, rebukes the spirit it came from, and rebukes them of ignorance of their own spirit; 'Ye know not what spirit ye are of'. As much to say as, If ye did, ye would make no such motions; that you do make any such, it proceeds from 'ye know not'. That would be marked. They are in ignorance, and the worst ignorance of themselves, that move for fire. They knew not what spirit they are of; but whatsoever it is, a wrong spirit it is, for here it is rebuked by Christ.

That which Christ rebuketh is 'ye know not', that is their fault; there is no word on which his rebuke can fall but that. It can be no good motion that comes from 'ye know not'. For from 'ye know not' cometh no good; without knowledge, the soul itself is not good. 'Ye know not what ye ask' – no good prayer. 'Ye know not what ye worship' – no good worship. And so ignorant devotion, implicit faith, blind obedience, all rebuked. Zeal, if it be not 'according to knowledge', cannot be 'according to conscience'; matter of conceit it may be, of conscience it cannot be. [. . .]

And it is not every ignorance, this: not of the act, but of the 'spirit' He chargeth, which is more. For 'God weighs the spirit'. Men look to the acts, He to the spirit; therefore try the act, but the spirit rather. We may be deceived in any act, if we know not the spirit it comes from. One and the same act proceeding from diverse spirits, good for one, for another not so. Therefore 'try the spirits' is ever good counsel, and 'discerning of spirits' a principal part of knowledge.

And if this import us to do in other men's spirits, not to be deceived in them, much more in our own; that we deceive not ourselves, which is the third degree. 'Ye know not of whose spirit ye are'; the foul elench of all, by ignorance of the true spirit, to fall into this 'error'. For indeed, many blind actions come from men by reason of ignorance of this third. And this we are to look to the rather, for that we see two so great Apostles like to precipitate themselves into a bloody act, for mistaking this point.

There are sure many 'ye know not' they were in. Elias, first, did not that they would do; that is one. His fire took hold of none but delinquents, every one as deep in the same fault as another. Here is a great many women and children in the town, not accessory to this. God would not suffer the wicked and innocent to perish together, no not in Sodom; would not suffer Nineveh to be destroyed, because there were in it that 'knew not their right hand from their left'. This did not Elias.

Then, it was but 'what Elias did', not 'as'; there is another. For what Elias did he did by special inspiration; had a particular commission, and as it were a privy seal for it. And that we must ever distinguish in the Prophets, when they proceed by their general calling, (therein we may follow them) and when an act is executed and done by them by immediate warrant; for such warrant passes not the person, no precedent to be made of it. Else, without their revelation, we may do 'what Elias did', and not 'as'. And that is a great 'ye know not', and doth much harm; for many a lewd attempt it is sought, and if they get it once over their heads, they think they are safe. For killing of Kings, 'as did Ehud'; of Queens, 'as did Jehoiada', for rebelling, 'as did Libna'. No, no; 'what he did', not 'as he did'; what they did they do, as they did they do not.

But if it were 'as did' too, it would not serve; it is a 'ye know not' still, and this is our Saviour Christ's, directed to their allegations of Elias. I observe they ask of the act, and Christ answers of the spirit. So that 'as did Elias', is not enough, is but a weak warrant; you must be of his spirit as well as do his act. His 'as' will not bear your act, unless you have his spirit too. It is not enough to say, 'as did Elias', unless you add, I am of the same spirit.

Then it remains, they must say they are of Elias' spirit, and into some such fancy it seems they were fallen; but that is another 'ye know not'. Why, what harm is that? Elias' spirit, I hope, was no evil spirit. No; but every good spirit, as good as Elias', is not for every person, place, or time. Spirits are given by God, and men inspired with them after several manners, upon several occasions, as the several times require. The times sometime so require one spirit, sometime another; Elias' time, Elias' spirit. As his act good, done by his spirit, so his spirit good in his own time. The time changed, the spirit then good, now not good. For both are faulty; the act without the spirit, and the spirit without the time. And so it may fall out that at some time one may be rebuked for being of Elias' spirit well enough, when Elias' spirit is out of time.

But why is it out of time? That is another 'ye know not', which Christ sets down plainly when He renders the reason, 'For the Son of man is come': for we may well make a pause there. As if He should say, Indeed, there is 'a time to destroy', saith Solomon, Ecclesiastes the third chapter – that was under the Law, the 'fiery Law', as Moses calls it; then a fiery spirit would not be amiss, then was Elias' time. But now the 'Son of man is come' – 'Ye know not what manner of spirit ye are of'. The spirit of Elias was good till the Son of man came; but now He is come, the date of that spirit is expired. When the Son of man is come, the spirit of Elias must be gone. Now especially; for Moses and he resigned lately in the mount. Now no law-giver, no prophet, but Christ. Christ now, and His Spirit, to take place. You move out of time; will ye be of Elias' spirit, and the Son of man is come? A plain 'ye know not'.

Gunpowder Treason, sermon 3, vol. 4, pp. 250–52

Extreme regard for the letter of the Old Testament was followed by John Traske, a sectary who claimed power to give the Holy Spirit by the laying on of hands and to cure diseases by anointing. He asserted that

Christians were bound by the Jewish dietary laws, and adopted from one of his followers the belief that the seventh day was the true day of rest. He was called before the Star Chamber in 1619, when Andrewes condemned his opinions, following denunciation of the dietary laws by affirming the Christian observance of the first day of the week. The reference to Socrates is not to the ancient Greek philosopher, but to Socrates Scholasticus, a Greek Church historian of the fifth century AD.

That Christian men are bound to the Jew's Sabbath. I had thought he had held both to that and to the Sunday too: and if that be his opinion, then is he a flat Ebionite (one of the first heresies that ever was condemned), that made a piece of linsey-woolsey of Christian religion, as appeareth by Eusebius.

But if to no other but that of the Saturday, then is he 'a very christened Jew', a Maran, the worst sort of Jews that is.

The Apostle (among others), reckoning up divers others, concludes with the Sabbath; and immediately upon it adds, 'Which all are but shadows of things to come' (Sabbath and all); 'but the body is Christ'. The *body* had, the *shadow* to vanish: that 'which was to come', when it is come, to what end any figure of it? it ceaseth too. That to hold the 'shadow of the Sabbath' is to continue, is to hold 'Christ the body' is not yet come.

It hath ever been the Church's doctrine, that Christ made an end of all Sabbaths, by His Sabbath in the grave. That Sabbath was the last of them. And, that the Lord's Day presently came in place of it: The Lord's Day as, by the resurrection of Christ, declared to be the Christian Day; and from that very time (of Christ's resurrection) it began to be celebrated, as the Christian Man's Festival', saith Austin. For the Sabbath had reference to the old Creation: but in Christ 'we are a new creature'; a new creation by Him, and so to have a new Sabbath: and 'the old things have passed away'. No reference to the old, we.

'By whom He made the worlds', saith the Apostle of Christ: so, two worlds there were. The first, that ended at Christ's *passion*, saith Athanasius; and therefore then the sun without any eclipse, went out of itself. The second, which began with Christ's *resurrection*: and that day, the beginning (and so, the Feast) of them that are 'in Christ a new creature'.

It is deduced plainly.

The Gospels keep one word, all four: tell us, Christ rose the first day of the week.

The Apostles, they keep their meetings on that day: and Saint Luke keeps the very same word exactly, 'the first day of the week' (to exclude all error). On that day they were 'gathered together' that is, held their 'Assemblies'; to preach, to pray, to break bread, or celebrate 'the Lord's Supper, on the Lord's Day'; for these two only, the Day, and the Supper, have the epithet of 'the Lord's' in the Scriptures; to show 'the Lord's is alike to be taken in both.

This for the practice then.

If you will have it in precept: The Apostle gives it (and in the same word still), that against 'the first day of the week' the day of their Assembly, 'Every one should lay apart what God should move him to offer to the collection for the saints, and then offer it': which was so ever in use. That, the day of oblations. So have you it, in practice and in precept, both. Even till Socrates' time, who keeps the same word still.

This day, this 'first day of the week' came to have the name of 'the Lord's Day' in the Apostles' times, and is so expressly called then, by Saint John in the Revelation.

And that name, from that day to this, it hath holden still; which continuance of it, from the Apostle's age, may be deduced down, from Father to Father, even to the first Council of Nicea; and lower, I trust, we need not follow it. No doubt is made of it since then, by any that hath read anything.

I should hold you too long, to cite them in particular. I avow it on my credit, there is not any ecclesiastical writer in whom it is not to be found. [. . .]

A thing so notorious, so well known even to the heathen themselves, as it was (in the Acts of the Martyrs) ever a usual question of theirs (even of course) in their examining. 'What? Hold you the Sunday?' and their answer known; they all aver it, 'I am a Christian, I cannot intermit it': Not the Lord's Day in any wise. These are examples enough.

Two Answers to Cardinal Perron and Other Miscellaneous Works,
Oxford: J.H. Parker, 1854, pp. 91–3

He was equally forceful in defending the Anglican interpretation of the Bible as against the contemporary Roman. Thomas Stapleton (1535–98) was a Roman Catholic apologist; prebendary of Chichester under Mary I, who later worked in Catholic centres on the Continent. Andradius (Diegius Payva Dandrada) published a defence of the doctrine of the Council of Trent in 1580.

Now in the way of Christianity there is yet no difference between the papists and us; let us therefore see wherein we and they differ.

Because they build themselves on the word of God, and so do we, but of a diverse meaning; we must look therefore for a right way to the interpretation of the word.

And this is the main question between them and us: Who have the true means to interpret?

They have the Fathers, Councils, the Church and the Pope. We have not so. But as it is 'the scripture is of no private interpretation'; so to make it plain what we hold, we will first lay down these three grounds.

That as to the eunuch [instructed and baptized by Philip], so much more to us there is need of an interpreter.

That there is a certain and infallible interpretation; else if we were always uncertain, how should we build on the rock?

As we must take heed of private interpretation, not to distort the scriptures; as Hilary saith, 'not to devise a sense for scripture but to give it its proper sense'; so must we hold that God hath given the gift of interpretation, which gift is not given to any but those which are in the church, and of those not to the common sort of every private man, but to the learned. And seeing it is, 'to each man as God pleaseth', it is not to be restrained to some one bishop, as the gross papists do. But Stapleton when he had proved all that he could, yet at last he was fain to confess that God doth extraordinarily give this gift to others, as well to Amos a herdsman, as Jeremy a priest. But Andradius leaned to the other side, saying that the bishop must approve their gifts.

Now for the sense of the word. It is well said in law, that 'each small quiddity of the law is not the law', so say we, the letter is not the word of God, but the meaning, and that is it which we seek; and for the meaning Thomas Aquinas saith,

in a matter of faith or manners we must take the literal sense;

for other things we may make a tropological sense;

there is but one true sense of one place;

that is it which the construction will give, if there follow no absurdity.

Now for the examination of the sense, because we must never look to stop their mouths, but they will still wrangle, we must therefore bring them to one of these;

to that, 'being condemned of himself' to drive them to condemn themselves in their own heart;

because the devil so blindeth some that they will not understand, therefore the second thing we must drive them to is that 'madness' be manifest.

Of our means of interpretation

The means for interpretation as we allege them, are six.

The first, wherein they and we agree, is prayer: so saith Augustine, 'prayer requesteth, reading searcheth, meditation findeth, contemplation directs'.

The second, third, and fourth, are for the phrase of speech:

Conference of places, the less plain must be referred to the more plain 'they searched the scriptures daily, whether those things were so; therefore many of them believed'.

'To look to the original', as, for the New Testament, the Greek text; for the Old, the Hebrew;

The acquaintance with the manner of dialect, that we may know the Holy Ghost's tongue, having our 'senses exercised to discern'.

The two last are for the word; the two following for the whole sentence and chapters.

That which they call 'the eye intent to the scope', 'avoiding profane and vain babblings, and oppositions of science falsely so called'; mark the end of the writer; for so saith Hilary, 'by finding the cause why a thing is spoken, we attain the understanding of that which learned men spake'.

To look to what goes before and what follows, with every circumstance.

And for these means we must note, that they are to be referred diversely to divers things, some to one and some to another, and not all to everything. And therefore Stapleton in reproving these means committed a double error; first, because he saw that some one of these was not necessary to some one thing, he thence concluded that it was not necessary at all; and secondly, because he saw that to something none of these severally could serve, he thereupon concluded that they were not at all sufficient.

Pattern of Catechetical Doctrine, pp. 57–9

8

Church and Ministry

Andrewes strongly defended the apostolic descent of the ordained ministry and the claim of the Church of England to full catholicity. The Church continues to exercise the authority and power given to the Apostles.

This power even in the Apostles' time was necessary: for God chargeth not His church with superfluous burdens; yet had they such graces (as power of healing, doing signs, sundry languages, &c) that they of all other might seem best able to want it, for by these graces they purchased both admiration and terror sufficient for crediting their bare word in the whole church. If necessary then in their times that were so furnished, much more in the ages ensuing, when all those graces ceased, and no means but it to keep things in order; so that were it not apparent to have been in the Apostles', yet the necessity of the times following, destitute of these helps, might enforce it.

Seeing then God hath no less care for the propagation and continuance of His Church for the first settling or planting of it, it must needs follow that this power was not personal in the Apostles, as tied to them only, but a power given to the Church; and in them for their times resident, but not ending with them, as temporary, but common to the ages after and continuing, to whom it was more needful than to them, to repress schism and to remedy other abuses.

So that the very same power at this day remaineth in the Church, and shall to the world's end.

A Pattern of Catechistical Doctrine, p. 356

At St Giles, Cripplegate, 9 January 1592

They continued steadfastly in the Apostles' doctrine and fellowship, and in breaking of bread, and in prayers.

Acts 2.42

'St Peter's wrench' refers to 'Things hard to be understood, which they that are unlearned and unstable wrest, as they do also the other scriptures, unto their own destruction.'

2 Peter 3.16

He maintains the necessity of bishops as successors of the Apostles and a distinct order in the Church, as against those who saw the episcopate only as a higher office for the priesthood or who wished totally to abolish it.

Now it is plain, there can no society endure without government, and therefore God hath appointed in it governors and assistants, which seeing they have power from God to reject or 'receive accusations', and to 'judge those that are within' and of the fellowship, it is an idle imagination that some have imagined, to hold 'the Church' hath not her judgement-seat, and power to censure her disobedient children. It hath ever been holden good divinity that the Church from Christ received power to censure and separate wilful offenders. Both, with the heathen man's separation, who might not so much as enter into the Church door, (which is the greater censure); and with the publican's separation, (which is the less) who might enter and pray in 'the temple', but was avoided in common conversation, and in the fellowship of the private table, and therefore much more of the altar. Of which twain, the former the Apostle calleth 'cutting off'; the latter, 'abstaining from'. The Primitive Church calleth the former *excommunicatos*, the latter *abstentos*. So that, to fancy no government, is an imagination. A government there is.

Touching the form of which government many imaginations have lately been bred in these our days especially. At the writing of this verse, it is certain that the government of Christian people consisted in two degrees only – of both which our Saviour Christ Himself was the Author: of the Twelve, [and] of the Seventy; both which were over the people, in things pertaining to God.

These two were, one superior to another, and not equal. And that the

Apostles established an equality in the Clergy, is, I take it, an imagination. No man could perish in the 'gainsaying of Korah' under the Gospel, which St Jude saith they may, if there were not a superiority in the Clergy; for Korah's mutiny was, because he might not be equal to Aaron, appointed his superior by God. Which very humour, observe it who will, hath brought forth most part of the heresies since the time of the Gospel; that Korah might not be Aaron's equal. Now of these two orders, the Apostles have ever been reckoned the superior to the other, till our times; as having, even under our Saviour Christ, a power to forbid others. And after, exercising the same power; Silas, one of the Seventy, receiving a commandment, from St Paul an Apostle to come unto him. As the auditory had their 'room' by themselves, so among the persons ecclesiastical the Apostles had a higher seat, as may be gathered; and in the very place itself were distinguished. Now in the place of the Twelve, succeeded Bishops; and in the place of the Seventy, Presbyters, Priests or Ministers, and that by the judgement of Irenaeus, who lived immediately upon the Apostles' age, of Tertullian, of St Augustine. And this, till of late, was thought the form of fellowship, and never other imagined.

But not long since, some have fancied another, that should consist of Lay-elders, Pastors, and Doctors, and whether of Deacons too is not fully agreed yet. Which device is pressed now upon our Church, not as a form of more convenience than that it hath, but as one absolutely necessary, and of our Saviour Christ's own only institution, which maketh it the less sufferable. I know that by virtue of St Peter's wrench before mentioned some places may be brought which may seem to give it colour, but that is if we allow those new glossed senses. But if we seek what senses the Primitive Church gave of them, not one of them but will suffer it to fall to the ground. And finding it a stranger to them, I know not how to term it but an imagination.

Certain sermons 2, vol. 5, pp. 62–4

Another argument for apostolic institution and example

That the churches thus planted and watered might so continue, the apostles ordained overseers to have a general care over the churches instead of themselves who first had the same; which is called *episkepsis* and continueth in it, as strengthening and establishing that which is already well, so a rectifying or redressing if ought be defective or amiss. These are called *episcopi*; by St John, the 'angels of the churches'. These were set over others, both to rule and teach. Upon these was transferred the chief part of the apostolic function, the oversight of the church; and power of commanding, correcting, and ordaining.

The occasion which caused the apostles to appoint bishops, besides the pattern in the time of the law, seemeth to have been schisms [. . .] for which St Cyprian, St Jerome, and all the fathers take the respect to one governor to be an especial remedy.

This power even in the apostles' time was necessary; for God chargeth not His church with superfluous burdens; yet had they such graces (as power of healing, doing signs, sundry languages, etc) that they of all others might seem best able to want it, for by those graces they purchased both admiration and terror sufficient for crediting their bare word in the whole church. If necessary then in their times that they were so furnished, much more in the ages ensuing, when all these graces ceased, and no means but it to keep things in order; so that were it not apparent to have been in the apostles', yet the necessity of the times following, destitute of these helps, might enforce it.

Seeing then that God has no less care for the propagation and continuance of His church than for the first settling or planting of it, it must needs follow that this power was not personal in the apostles, as tied to them only, but a power given to the church; and in them for their times resident, but not ending with them as temporary, but common to the ages after and continuing, to whom it was more needful than to them, to repress schism and to remedy other abuses.

So that the very same power at this day remaineth in the church, and shall to the world's end.

A Pattern of Catechetical Doctrine, pp. 355–6

At Whitehall on the Sunday after Easter, 13 March 1600

Whosesoever sins ye remit, they are remitted unto them; and whosesoever sins ye retain, they are retained.

John 20.23

In this sermon 'Of the Powers of Absolution' he defends sacramental confession and the priestly power of absolution, both supported in the

Book of Common Prayer. He speaks of the 'Ministry of reconciliation' (2 Corinthians 5.18), a description largely revived in the Church today.

The power of remitting sin is originally in God, and in God alone. And in Christ our Saviour, by means of the union of the Godhead and manhood into one person; by virtue whereof 'the Son of man hath power to forgive sins upon earth'.

This power being thus solely invested in God He might without wrong to any have retained and kept to Himself, and without means of word or Sacrament, and without Ministers, either Apostles or others, have exercised immediately by Himself from heaven.

But we should then have said of the remission of sins, saith St Paul, 'Who shall go up to heaven for it, and fetch it thence?' For which cause, saith he, 'the righteousness of faith speaketh thus, Say not so in thy heart. The word shall be near thee, in thy mouth, and in thy heart, and this is the word of faith which we preach'.

Partly this, that there should be no such difficulty to shake our faith, as once to imagine to fetch Christ from heaven for the remission of our sins.

Partly also, because Christ, to Whom alone this commission was originally granted, having ordained Himself a body, would work by bodily things; and having taken the nature of man upon Him, would honour the nature He had so taken. For these causes, that which was His and His alone He vouchsafed to impart; and out of His commission to grant a commission, and thereby to associate them to Himself – it is His own word by the Prophet – and to make them 'workers together with Him', as the Apostle speaketh, to the work of salvation both of themselves and of others.

From God then it is derived; from God, and to men.

To men, and not to Angels. And this I take to be a second prerogative of our nature. That an Angel must give order to Cornelius to send to Joppa for one Simon, to speak words to him by which he and his household should be saved, but the Angel must not be the doer of it. That not to Angels, but to men, is committed this office or embassage of reconciliation. And that which is yet more, to sinful men, for so is the truth, and so themselves confess it. St Peter: 'Go from me, Lord, for I am a sinful man'. St James: 'In many things we offend all'; putting himself in the number. And, lest we should think it to be but their modesty, St John speaketh plainly: 'If we say we have no sin' – what then? not, we are proud, and there is no humility in us, but, 'we are liars, and there is no truth in us'. And this is that which is wonderful in this point, that St Paul who confesseth himself 'a sinner' and 'a chief sinner', 'of whom I am chief'; the same concerning another sinner, the incestuous Corinthian, 'I forgive it him', saith he, 'in the person of Christ'.

Now if we ask to what men? the text is plain. They to whom Christ said this 'Ye remit', were the Apostles.

In the Apostles, that we may come nearer yet, we find three capacities, as we may term them: as Christians in general; as Preachers, Priests, or Ministers, more special; as those twelve persons, whom in strict propriety of speech we term the Apostles.

Some things that Christ spake to them, He spake to them as representing the whole company of Christians, as His 'Watch'.

Some things to them, not as Christians, but as preachers or Priests as His 'Go and preach the Gospel', and His 'Do this', which no man thinketh all Christians may do.

And some things to themselves personally; as that He had appointed them 'witnesses' of His miracles and resurrection, which cannot be applied but to them, and them in person. It remaineth we enquire, in which of these three capacities Christ imparteth to them this commission.

Not as to Apostles properly. That is, this was no personal privilege to be in them and to die with them, that they should only execute it for a time, and none ever after them. God forbid we should so think it. For this power being more than needful for the world, as in the beginning it was said, it was not to be either personal or for a time. Then those persons dying, and those times determining, they in the ages following, as we now in this, that should light into this prison or captivity of sin, how could they or we receive any benefit by it? Of nature it is said by the heathen philosopher, that it doth neither 'abound in superfluity', nor 'be lacking in necessity'. God forbid but we should ascribe as much to God at the least that neither He would ordain a power superfluous or more than needed, or else it being needful would appropriate it unto one age, and leave all other destitute of it; and not rather as all writers both new and old take it, continue it successively to the world's end.

And as not proper to the Apostles' persons, so neither common to all Christians in general, nor in the persons of all Christians conveyed to them. Which thing, the very circumstance of the text do evict. For He sent them first, and after inspired them; and after both these, gave them this commission. Now all Christians are not so sent, nor are all Christians inspired with the grace or gift of the Spirit that they were here. Consequently, it was not intended to the whole society of Christians. Yea I add, that forasmuch as these two, both these two, must go before it, 'Sending', and 'Inspiring', that though God inspire some laymen, if I may have leave so to term them, with very special graces of knowledge to this end, yet inasmuch as they have not the former of sending, it agreeth not to them, neither may they exercise it until they be sent, that is, until they have their calling thereunto.

It being then neither personal nor peculiar to them as Apostles, nor again common to all as Christians, it must needs be committed to them as Ministers, Priests, or Preachers, and consequently to those that in that office and function do succeed them, to whom and by whom this commission is still continued. Neither are they that are ordained or instituted to that calling, ordained or instituted by any other words or verse than this. Yet not so that absolutely without them God cannot bestow it on whom or when Him pleaseth, or that He is bound to this means only, and cannot work without it. For, 'the grace of God is not bound but free', and can work without means either of word or Sacrament; and as without means, so without Ministers how and when to Him seemeth good. But speaking of that which is proper and ordinary in the course by Him established this is an Ecclesiastical act committed, as the residue of the ministry of reconciliation, to Ecclesiastical persons. And if at any time He vouchsafe it by others that are not such, they be in that case 'in case of necessity Ministers, but by office not so.'

Now as by committing this power God doth not deprive or bereave Himself of it, for there is a 'They are remitted' still, and that chief, sovereign, and absolute; so on the other side where God proceedeth by the Church's act as ordinarily He doth, it being His own ordinance, there whosoever will be partaker of the Church's act must be partaker of it by the Apostles' means; there doth 'Ye remit' concur in his own order and place, and there runneth still a correspondence between both. There doth God associate His Ministers, and maketh them 'workers together with Him'. There have they their parts in this work, and cannot be excluded; no more in this than in the other acts and parts of their function. And to exclude them is, after a sort, to wring the keys out of their hands to whom Christ hath given them, is to cancel and make void this clause of 'Ye remit', as if it were no part of the sentence; to account of all this solemn sending and inspiring, as if it were an idle and fruitless ceremony; which if it may not be admitted, then sure it is they have their part and concurrence in this work, as in the rest of 'the ministry of reconciliation'.

Certain sermons . . . upon several occasions 4, vol. 5, pp. 90–93

The best-known exposition of principles for the character and behaviour of the clergy is probably George Herbert's A Priest to the Temple, *and others followed in the seventeenth and eighteenth centuries. Andrewes, with his high and solemn view of priesthood, wrote one of the earliest Anglican statements of ideals, 'The character and duties of a minister of the Gospel'. In the controversial condition of the time, his demand for a learned and disciplined clergy was particularly apposite.*

One good kind of minister

Now the good shepherd, he it is only that performeth his duty; and the duty of the good shepherd may be reduced to these four heads.

His duties: first, to be an example in his life.

To go before his sheep, as the manner of the east countries was, not to drive his sheep but to go before them; the good shepherd must go before his flock by his good example, he must be *tupos* [a pattern] that is, such a thing as maketh the stamp upon the coin [. . .] And Moses requireth he should have *thummin* 'integrity of life', as well as *urim*, 'light' of learning, And it is said of our Saviour Christ, our *tupos* He 'began to do and teach'; so the minister must do first and teach after; he must be an example unreproveable, and unblameable.

And this must be in him, and his.

In himself, 'without spot', not misshapen, or having blemish, that is to say, any notorious sin or crime that is outward, to be laid to his charge; and the reason is that there may be no offence given to the weak, or slander to the gospel, by the wicked, but that even the enemies may by his example become, Christians.

In his household, that is, in his charge; those that are committed to him; that is, if he be a prophet, in the church; if a father, in his sons; if a master, in his servants. And this standeth in these points:

Those that be under him must be religious and faithful children; 'faithful children, not accused of riot, or unruly';
they must be under obedience; 'in subjection'; or else it is a presumption of negligence, faintheartedness, or carelessness in him;
they must use reverence, gravity, modesty; they must be no rioters, drunkards, or such like.

The duty of the people, answerable to this example of the shepherd, is to follow his example; if he must be 'a pattern to his flock', they must be an 'imprint of the shepherd', as in the print of the coin, the iron and the coin are of the same figure.

Secondly, to teach by his learning.

As he must be an example and go before them in life, so he must also teach and instruct them by learning; and therefore must be 'able to teach'.

It is well observed that the verb 'to teach', doth govern two accusative cases, as 'whom' he will teach knowledge; they must have: 'whom' they should teach, and 'what' they shall teach, namely, knowledge. Many have 'a people to teach', but have not 'knowledge to teach them', and so they are not teachers sent from God, but thieves and robbers sent by the devil. God Himself saith to such unlearned priests, 'because thou hast refused knowledge, I have refused thee that thou shalt be no priest unto Me'.

And to enquire what measure of knowledge is needful for him to have, the schoolmen say he must have 'competent' if not 'knowledge in an eminent degree'; and what competent knowledge is, we may see in these three points; he must be able to

hold fast the faithful word according to knowledge;
exhort and comfort, and that with wholesome doctrine;
improve and confute them that say against it.

Thirdly, to have a care of the manner of his doctrine.

As he must be an example in his life, and teach them by his learning, so he must have a care of the manner of his doctrine, in what sort he doth teach.

We read of three faults that fell into the church in the apostle's time;
'a desire to hear fables'; when a man is soon full, and cannot abide to hear of a thing often, but will have new; they must have 'another Jesus, another Saviour';

they did 'talk emptily', they must 'have questions to no profit', and decidings of high and nice points;

they had 'itching ears', a desire to hear an eloquent declamation out of a pulpit; to have a period fall roundly, pleasing the ear, and doing the soul no good.

Against these the apostle setteth down a form for the preacher to follow;

that which he teacheth must be wholesome and uncorrupt doctrine, he must not meddle with things of no profit, but he must intend the people's good by his preaching;

for the delivery it must be with learning; 'though rude in speech, yet not in know ledge'; and he must not only have 'old matters' but 'new'; not new doctrine, but new ways of expressing, and new arguments.

and he must also use a plain and perspicuous order, and an orderly delivering of it, which is called 'a dividing of the word aright';

and according to that, 'the word is a two-edged sword', it is a special point in preaching that their words must have two edges, for else the back commonly doth as much harm as the edge doth good. And that is when they did not meet with both extremes; as when they speak of obedience, they deal as if they would take away all disobedience, and would have man never to disobey; and when they speak of peace, they do it so as if we should have peace with all men and be at variance with none; whereas with the wicked we must have no peace;

and lastly, the minister must deliver the word with authority, gravity, and majesty; as knowing that it is not his own word, but the everlasting truth of God.

Fourthly, to reprove and confute.

As he must be of good life, and sufficient learning to teach, and must teach them after a right and good order; so with his teaching them that which is good, he must reprove the offenders, and improve and confute them that are contrary minded.

For the manner of his reproving, he must

first 'prove' the fault, and then 'reprove' it; and, in regard of the person offending,

if they be only led by a disposition to a fault, then 'in humility';

if it be done in contempt, then 'with all authority';

if the parties be forward of nature then 'roundly and sharply';

if it be a public fault, then reprove him roundly, that others may fear.

For improving or confuting the adversary,

if it may be, to stop his mouth;

if that cannot be, yet that he may be confounded;

if not that, yet that inwardly he may be convinced in his conscience, 'condemned of himself'; if that will not be, yet that his madness may be made manifest, and the hearers may see his folly.

The people's duty in respect of all this pains of the minister is, to yield him 'double honour', as it is

the honour of reverence, both in judgement and in affection.

the honour of maintenance, to make them partakers of all our goods.

A Pattern of Catechistical Doctrine, pp. 194–8

9

Faith and Works

Although Andrewes held to the Reformation doctrine of the total neces-
sity of faith and the insufficiency of works to procure salvation, one of
his strongest tenets was the duty of perseverance and an active response
to the faith professed. He taught it from his early to his latest work; it is
included in his sermon on the Magi (p. 26) and is developed in many
other places. These passages show his regard for both faith and personal
endeavour.

We cannot come to God save by belief.

Now to show that there is no other way to come to God, but belief.

If they should in any manner be driven to prove everything by reason,
it would drive them into madness.

No man can make demonstration of everything, no not in matters of
the world; a man cannot make a demonstration that his father is his
father, or that he is his son; so that there must needs be belief.

If a man should say he hath seen such and such a place, he can make
no demonstrative reason of it; for the circumstances are not capable of
demonstration, and no more is God, being the end of our journey.

Thus much for the necessity of belief; now for the belief itself.

'A learner must believe'; must lay hold of that we hear; but this belief
at the first is not perfect, 'for that which is received in an imperfect body
is at the first imperfect'; wood in the fire is first warm before it burn; it
hath 'heat from another', before it have 'its own' heat; so the learner
must first take 'of another man's credit'; 'unless you believe ye shall not
be established'.

We must try and prove those things which we receive, either 'by what
is precedent or consequent', 'for we have inbred in us the principles, as
of other virtues, so of religion'; and reason uncorrupt always agreeth
with God's word, and so God sends us often to nature; so the Apostle

'the invisible things from the creation of the world are clearly seen, being understood by the things that are made'.

When we have thus strengthened our faith, we must yet look for a higher teacher; for though faith be a perfect way, yet we walk unperfectly in it, and therefore 'in things above nature we must believe God only;' so that we must look to God for His spirit and inspiration.

This inspiration cometh not at the first, and therefore we must, as they say, 'make haste with leisure', to avoid rashness; as Esay, 'he that believes maketh not haste', so we must wax perfect by little and little, and ever be building 'to our faith, virtue; to our virtue, knowledge; to our knowledge, temperance; with temperance, patience; with patience, godliness; with godliness, brotherly kindness; with brotherly kindness, love', and though we build slowly, yet ever be sure to build on the rock.

Of perseverance

Now for perseverance. The answer to, 'thou shalt have no other gods' is not 'I have no other', but 'I will have no other'. These verbs of time, 'I was', 'I am', 'I shall be', may all work in us a fear to see what we have been, what we are, and what we shall be, especially because we know not whether God will forsake us or not.

Perseverance is distinguished from patience, in that the object of patience is 'the sorrow of bearing the cross', and the object of perseverance is 'the tediousness of long delay'.

Here are condemned:

Those that persevere and continue in a evil thing, rise early that they may follow strong drink, that continue until night, till wine inflame them; 'they that tarry long at the wine'.

Those that do at once fall quite away, or if not, yet are wavering and unsteadfast, as Pharaoh was.

Means to perseverance

As in patience, to prepare ourselves against our enemies.
To set much by religion, for if we set little by it we shall not continue;
To desire not to run in vain;
To consider the continuance of the reward, which shall last for ever.

Signs of perseverance

Not to look back but forward, 'never to say, it is enough', for 'when you cease to be better, you begin to be worse'; as they that row against the stream, if they hold still, are carried backward.

That which is, 'I know thy works, and charity, and service, and faith, and thy patience, and thy works; and the last to be more than the first'; if our last fruit be more than our first; and if we 'grow from strength to strength'; if our 'love may abound more and more in knowledge and in all judgement'.

A Pattern of Catechistical Doctrine, pp. 21–2, 121–2

Before Queen Elizabeth I at Hampton Court, 6 March 1594

Remember Lot's wife.

Luke 17.32

After preaching the need for continual vigilance and perseverance, he ends with a panegyric of the Queen as a model of these qualities. Ecebolius was a Christian who returned to pagan philosophy under Julian the Apostate.

Remember, we be not weary to go whither God would have us – not to Zoar, though a little one, if our soul may there live; and never buy the ease of our body, with the hazard of our soul, or a few days of vanity with the loss of eternity.

Remember, we slack not our pace, nor stand still on the plain. For if we stand still, by still standing we are meet to be made a pillar, even to stand still, and never to remove.

Remember, we look not back, either with her on the vain delights of Sodom left; or with Peter on St John behind us, to say, 'Lord, what shall this man do'? both will make us forget our following. 'None that casteth his eye the other way', is 'meet' as he should be, 'meet for the Kingdom of God'.

But specially remember we leave not our heart behind us, but that we take that with us, when we go out of Sodom; for if that stay, it will stay the feet, and writhe the eye, and neither the one nor the other will do their duty. Remember, that our heart wander not, that our heart long not. This care, if it be fervent, will bring us perseverance.

Now, that we may the better learn somewhat out of her punishment too; let us remember also, that as to her, so to us, God may send some unusual visitation, and take us suddenly away, and in the act of sin too.

Remember the danger and damage; it is no less matter we are about, than 'to lose one's soul'. Which if we do, we frustrate and forfeit all the fruit of our former well-continued course; all we have done is vain. Yea, all that Christ hath done for us is in vain; Whose pains and sufferings we ought specially to tender, knowing that 'no labour to lost labour'; and Christ then hath lost His labour for us.

Remember the folly; that 'beginning in the Spirit' we 'end in the flesh'; turning our backs to Zoar, we turn our face to Sodom; joining to a head of fine gold feet of clay, and to a precious foundation a covering of thatch.

Remember the disgrace; that we shall lose our credit and account while we live, and shall hear that of Christ, 'This man'; and that other, 'What went ye into the desert to see? A reed shaken with the wind?'

Remember the scandal; that, falling ourselves, we shall be a block for to make others fall; a sin no lighter, nor less, nor lighter than a millstone.

Remember the infamy; that we shall leave our memory remaining in stories, among Lot's wife, and Job's wife, Demas and Ecebolius, and the number of relapsed, there to stand to be pointed at, no less than this heap of salt.

Remember the judgement that is upon them after their relapse, though they live, that they do even with her here 'wax hard and numb,' and serve others for a caveat, wholly unprofitable for themselves.

Remember the difficulty of reclaiming to good; 'seven evil spirits entering instead of one, that their 'last state is worse than the first'.

And lastly, Remember that we shall justify Sodom by so doing, and her frozen sin shall condemn our melting virtue. For they in the wilfulness of their wickedness persisted till fire from Heaven consumed them; and they being thus obdurate in sin, ought not she, and we much more, to be constant in virtue? And if the drunkard hold out till he have lost his eyes, the unclean person till he have wasted his loins, the contentious till he have consumed his wealth, 'What shame is it, that God's unhappy people should not be as constant in virtue, as these miscreants have been, and be in vice!'

Each of these by itself, all these put together will make a full memento, which if she had remembered, she had been a pillar of light in

Heaven, not of salt in earth. It is too late for her – we in due time yet may remember it.

And when we have remembered these, remember Christ too that gave the memento; that He calleth Himself Alpha and Omega – not only Alpha for His happy beginning, but Omega for His thrice happy ending. For that He left us not, nor gave over the work of our redemption, till He brought it to 'It is finished'. And that on our part, 'the highest act of religion, is for the Christian to conform himself, not to Lot's wife, but to Christ, Whose name he weareth'. And though 'true love indeed receiveth no manner strength from hope', but, though it hope for nothing, loveth nevertheless; yet to quicken our love, which oft is but faint, and for a full memento, remember the reward. Remember how Christ will remember us for it; which shall not be the wages of an hireling, or lease-wise for time, and term of years, but 'throughout all ages', eternity itself, never to expire, end, or determine, but to last and endure for ever and ever.

But this reward, saith Ezekiel, is for those, whose foreheads are marked with Tau, which, as Omega in Greek, is the last letter in the Hebrew alphabet, and the mark of 'It is finished' among them; they only shall escape the wrath to come. And this crown is laid up for them, not of whom it may be said, 'ye did run well'; but for those that can say with St Paul, 'I have finished my course well'.

And, thanks be to God, we have not hitherto wanted this salt, but remembered Lot's wife well. So that this exhortation, because we have prevented and done that which it calleth for, changeth his nature and becometh a commendation, as all others do. A commendation I say; yet not so much of the people, whose only felicity is to serve and be subject to one that is constant – for otherwise we know how wavering a thing the multitude is – as of the Prince, whose constant standing giveth strength to many a weak knee otherwise. And blessed be God and the Father of our Lord Jesus Christ, that we stand in the presence of such a Prince, who hath ever accounted of perseverance, not only as of 'the Queen of virtues', but as of 'the virtue of a Queen.' Who, like Zerubbabel, first by princely magnanimity laid the corner-stone in a troublesome time; and since, by heroical constancy, through many both alluring proffers and threatening dangers, hath brought forth the Headstone also with the Prophet's acclamation, 'Grace, grace, unto it' – Grace, for so happy a beginning, and Grace for so thrice happy an ending. No terrors, no enticement, no care of her safety hath removed her from her steadfastness; but with a fixed eye, with straight steps, with a resolute mind, hath entered herself, and brought us into Zoar. It is a little one, but therein our souls shall live; and we are in safety, all the cities of the plain being in combustion round about us. Of whom it shall be remembered, to her high praise, that all her days she served God 'with a covenant of salt', and with her Israel, from the first day until now. And of this be we persuaded, that 'He which began this good work in her, will perform it unto the day of Jesus Christ', to her everlasting praise, comfort, and joy, and in her to the comfort, joy, and happiness of us all.

Yet it is not needless, but right requisite, that we which are the Lord's remembrancers put you in mind, that as perseverance is the queen of virtues, 'for she alone is crowned'; so it is also 'for that all Satan's malice and his practices are against it'. The more careful need we to be, to carry in our eye this example. Which God grant we may, and that our hearts may seriously regard, and our memories carefully keep it, 'that this pillar may prop our weakness, and this salt season our sacrifice', that it may be remembered, and accepted, and rewarded in the day of the Lord!

Lent Sermon 4, vol. 2, pp. 73–7

Before Elizabeth I at Greenwich, 24 February 1590

Thou leddest Thy people like a flock by the hand of Moses and Aaron.

Psalm 77.20

Elaborate and almost Metaphysical reflections on 'hands' as God's power and as human instruments to perform his will. Nazianzen: St Gregory of Nazianzus (329–89) theologian, one of the Cappadocian Fathers.

First, the Prophet calleth God's hands, by whom He leadeth us; and secondly telleth us who they be – Moses and Aaron.

God's hands they be; for that by them He reacheth unto us, and in it religion and counsel and justice and victory, and whatsoever else is good. 'He sendeth His word to Moses first, and by him' as it were through his hand, 'His statutes and ordinances unto all Israel'.

And not good things only, but if they so deserve, sometimes evil also. For as, if they be virtuous, such as Moses and Aaron, they be the 'good hand' of God for our benefit, such as was upon Ezra; so if they be evil, such as Balak and Balaam, they be the 'heavy hand' of God for our chastisement, such as was upon Job. But the hand of God they be both. And a certain resemblance there is between this government and the hand; for as we see the hand itself parted into divers fingers, and those again into sundry joints, for the more convenient and speedy service thereof; so is the estate of government; for ease and expedition, branched into the middle offices, and they again as fingers into others under them. But the very meanest of them all, is a joint of some finger of this hand of God. Nazianzen, speaking of rulers as of the images of God, compareth the highest to pictures drawn clean through, even to the feet; the middle sort to half pictures drawn but to the girdle; the meanest to the lesser sort of pictures drawn but to the neck or shoulders. But all in some degree carry the image of God.

Out of which term, of 'the hands of God', the people first are taught their duty, so to esteem of them, as of God's own hands; that as God ruleth them by 'the hands of Moses and Aaron', that is by their ministry, so Moses and Aaron rule them by the hands of God, that is, by His authority. It is His name they wear, it is His seat they sit in, it is the rod of God that is in Moses' and Aaron's hands. If we fall down before them, it is He that is honoured; if we rise up against them, it is He that is injured; and that must be our confession, 'against Heaven and them', but first against Heaven and God Himself, when we commit any contempt against Moses or Aaron.

And the rulers have their lesson too. First, that if they be God's hands, then His Spirit is to open and shut them, stretch them out, and draw them in, wholly to guide and govern them, as the hand of man is guided and governed by the spirit that is in man. Heavenly and divine had those hands need be, which are to be the hands and to work the work of God.

Again, they be not only hands, but hands in action. Not to be wrapped up in soft fur, but by which an actual duty of leading is to be performed. Moses' own hand, in the fourth of Exodus, when he had lodged it in his warm 'bosom, became leprous'; but being stretched out, recovered again. Hands in action then they must be; not loosely hanging down or folded together in idleness, but stretched out; not only to point others but themselves to be foremost in the execution of every good work.

Thirdly, 'hands by which they were led' that is, as not the 'leprous hand' of Moses, so neither the 'withered hand' of Jeroboam stretching itself out against God, by misleading His people and making them to sin. 'Leading back again into Egypt' – a thing expressly forbidden; either to the oppression and bondage of Egypt, or to the ignorance and false worship of Egypt, from whence Moses had led them. For as they be not entire bodies of themselves but hands, and that not their own but God's; so the people they led are not their own but His, and by Him and to Him to be led and directed. So much for 'God's hands'.

This honourable title of the 'hand of God' is here given to two parties, Moses and Aaron, in regard of two distinct duties performed by them. Ye heard how we said before, The people of God were like sheep in respect of a double want; want of strength by means of their feebleness; and want of skill by means of their simpleness. For this double want here cometh a double supply, from the hand of strength, and of cunning; for both these are in the hand.

It is of all members the chief in might, as appeareth by the diversity of uses and services it is put to. 'In the power of thy right hand', saith the Prophet.

And secondly, it is also the part of greatest cunning, as appeareth by the variety of the works which it yieldeth, by the pen, the pencil, the needle, and instruments of music. 'By the skill of his hands' saith the Psalmist, in the end of the next Psalm; and, 'let my right hand forget her cunning'.

This hand of God then by his strength affordeth protection to the feebleness of the flock, and again by his skill affordeth direction to the simpleness of the flock. And these are the two substantial parts of all leading.

Lent sermon 2, vol. 2, pp. 30–32

Before James I at Whitehall, Whitsunday, 27 May 1610

If ye love Me, keep My commandments.

John 14.15–16

Profession of love for God is empty unless it is proved by obedience. Of which every season in the years reminds us.

The condition stands first, as first commended to our care. For of our part we need have care; on His, we need not. And let me say this of it: no condition could have been devised more proper and fit for this feast – both parts of it. First, 'If you love Me' – 'love'; and this is 'the feast of love'; and He Whose the feast is, the Holy Ghost, love itself, the essential love and love-knot of the two Persons of the Godhead, Father and Son. The same, the love-knot between God and man, and yet more specially between Christ and His Church. Properly, as faith referreth to Christ the Word, so doth love to the Spirit, and comfort to love. It is the Apostle; 'If there be any comfort, it is in love'. What condition could be more fit?

And the second is like to it, as fit in every way: 'keep My Commandments'. For ye shall read in Exodus, that at the feast of Pentecost the commandments were given. The very Feast itself institute in remembrance of the Law then given: then very meet they be remembered of them at this Feast. And the Holy Ghost sent, among other things, that they may be written not in stone, but in their hearts; not with the letter, but with the Spirit; and the spirit not of fear, but love, as by Whom the love of God is shed abroad in our hearts. Which love is the fulfilling of the Commandments, and they all abridged in this one word 'you love'. So, whether we regard the Feast, or the Person, or the office of Him to Whom we hold the Feast, the condition is well chosen.

To begin then with the first; 'If ye love Me'. 'Love' is not so fit here, as 'if' is unfitting. For 'if' is as if there were some if, some doubt in the matter; whereof, God forbid there should be any. It would be without 'if'. Thus rather: 'forasmuch as you love Me, keep My Commandments'. That they and we love Him, I trust, shall not need to be put as a hypothesis; 'seeing He is so well worthy of our love', that we to blame, if we endure any 'if' any question to be made of it.

It grieveth me to stand long on this condition, to make an *if* of it at Pentecost. Take the feasts all along, and see if by every one of them 'it' be not put past 'if'. Christmas-day: for us, and for our love, He 'became flesh', that we might love Him, because like us He took our nature on Him. New year's-day: 'knowing no sin, He was made sin for us', sealed the bond with the first drops of His blood, wherewith the debt of our sin light upon Him. Candlemas-day: He was presented in the Temple, offered as a live oblation for us, that so the obedience of His whole life might be ours. Good Friday: made a slain sacrifice on the cross, that we might be redeemed by the benefit of His death. Easter-day: opened us the gate of life, 'as the first fruits of them' that rise again. Ascension-day: opened us the gate of Heaven; thither, 'our forerunner entered', to prepare a place for us. And this day seals up all by giving us seisin of all He hath done for us, by His Spirit sent down upon earth. And after all this, come ye in with 'If ye love me'? Shall we not strike out 'if', and make the condition absolute? Shall we not to St Paul's 'if', 'If any man love not the Lord Jesus, let him be *anathema maranatha*', [accursed] all say, let him be so?

'If we love them that love us, what singular thing do we, since the very Publicans do the like'? That if our love be but as the Publican's, there would be no 'if' made of it, for He loved us.

And not because we loved Him, but He loved us first. 'No more kindly attractive of love, than in loving to prevent; for too hard metal is he of, that though he like not to love first, will not requite it and love again, either first or second.'

Specially, since His love was not little, but such as St John makes 'see how great love'. How great? So, as none greater. 'For, greater love hath no man than this, to give his life for his friends'. No man greater but He, for His was beyond. To give His life, is but to die any sort of death; but 'by the death of the Cross', to die as. He died, that is more. And for such as were His friends is much, but, 'while we were yet sinners' is a great deal more. And yet is it 'If'? Put it to the Prophet's question, 'What should He have done' And add to it, if ye will, 'What should He have suffered'? What should He have done, and what suffered? If He did it not, if He suffered not, make an 'if' of His love; but if He did both, out with it.

But the Publican will be the Publican, and the world the world, their love is mercenary sale ware; no profit, no love. To take away that 'if', even thither He will follow us, and apply Himself to that. And if we will make port-sale of our love, and let it go by Who gives more? He will out-bid all. All, by the last word, 'to Eternity'. For whatsoever we may have here, if it were a kingdom, it is not for ever. But this 'Comforter' That 'shall abide with us', is but a pledge of that bliss and kingdom of His wherein we shall abide with Him eternally. Let any offer more for our love, and carry it.

Whitsun sermon 3, vol. 3, pp.147–9

Before James I at Greenwich, Whitsunday, 16 May 1619

He that feareth Him, and worketh righteousness, is accepted with Him.

Acts 10.34–5

One of his strongest sermons about the need for active obedience to God. Good works like alms, prayer and fasting must accompany faith.

He condemns passive religion, listening to sermons or 'lectures' instead of praying.

Wherefore, when the Gospel was at the highest, 'work out your salvation with fear and trembling', saith St Paul; 'pass the time of your dwelling here in fear', saith St Peter. Yea, our Saviour Himself, as noteth St Augustine, when He had taken away one fear, 'Fear not them that can kill the body, and when they have done that, have done all, and can do no more'; in place of that fear puts another, 'but fear Him That when He hath slain the body, can cast soul and it into hell fire'; and when He had so said once, comes over again with it to strike it home; 'Yea, I say unto you; fear Him'.

So then, this of fear is not Moses' song only, it is 'the song of Moses and the Lamb' both. Made of the harmony of the one as well as the other. A special strain in that 'song of Moses and the Lamb' you shall find this, 'Who will not fear Thee, O Lord?' He that will not may 'make himself music'; he is out of their choir, yea the Lamb's choir; indeed, out of both.

This have I a little stood on, for that, methinks, the world begins to grow from fear too fast: we strive to blow this Spirit quite away; for fear of the 'pangs of conscience', we seek to benumb it, and to make it past feeling. For these causes, fear is, with God, a thing acceptable, we hear; and that the Holy Ghost came down where this fear was, we see. So it is, St Peter affirms it 'for certain, of a truth': so it is, St Peter protests it. Let no man beguile you, to make you think otherwise. No, no; but 'Do it man, I tell thee, do it, though it be for fear of punishment, if you cannot get yourself to do it for love of righteousness'. One will bring on the other; 'By fear of the Lord we receive the Spirit of salvation' – it is Esay. By it we shall conceive that which shall save us. These very words shall save us, said the Angel, and so they did; here in Cornelius, we have a fair precedent for it. And so, now I come to the other.

For, I ask, is God all for within? accepts He of nothing without? Yes that He doth. Of a good righteous work too, if it proceed from His fear in our hearts. Fear is not all then: no, for it is but 'the beginning', as we have heard, righteousness will have us begin, but not end there. We have begun with 'who feareth Him', we must end with 'and worketh righteousness', and then comes 'is accepted with Him', and not before. For neither fear, if it be fear alone; nor faith, if it be faith alone, is accepted of Him; but 'feareth' and 'worketh' here with Peter, and 'and faith which worketh' there with Paul; fear and faith both that worketh, and none else. If it be true fear, if such as God will accept, it is not 'a dull lazy fear'; his fear that feared his Lord, and went and 'digged his talent into the ground', did nothing with it. Away with his fear and him 'into utter darkness'! God will have his talent turned, have it above ground. He will not have His religion invisible within. No; 'show me thy faith', saith St James; 'thy fear', saith St Peter here, by some works of righteousness. Else talk not of it. He will have it made appear, that men may see it, and glorify Him for it, that hath such good and faithful servants.

And they observe that it is not 'that doeth', but 'that worketh righteousness'. Not 'doeth' but 'worketh'. And what manner of work? St Peter's word is 'worketh righteousness' here; and for 'worketh righteousness', [simple] 'work' will not serve; it must be [productive] 'work' which is plain 'trade'. 'Learn to do well' saith Esay, learn it, as one would learn a handicraft, to live by; learn it, and be occupied in it; make an 'occupation' of it Christ's own occupation, Who, as St Peter tells us straight after, 'went up and down, went about doing good', practising it, and nothing else; for that is 'working righteousness'.

'Worketh righteousness'. This 'righteousness', to know what it is – besides the common duties of our calling, either as Christians in general; or particular, as every man's occupation lies – we cannot better inform ourselves of it, than from this party he speaks of from Cornelius, and what the works were he did. And they are set down at the second verse where, after St Luke has said, 'he feared God', to show his works of righteousness he adds, 'he gave much alms', and 'prayed to God continually'; and at the thirteenth verse, that he was found 'fasting at the ninth hour', that is, three at afternoon. In these three, 'alms', 'prayer', and 'fasting' stood his works of righteousness – in these three; for besides them we find not any other. They be the same, and in the same order, as they were figured in the three oblations of the Magi, firstfruits of the Gentiles, there in the Gospel, as the Fathers allot them: 'Gold', that is for 'alms'; 'incense', that is 'prayer'; and 'myrrh', bitter myrrh, for works of mortification, as 'fasting' and such like; as bitter to the flesh, as myrrh to the taste; both bitter, but wholesome both. But without all figure they are the same three, and stand just in the same order that here they do, where our Saviour teacheth them literally, and that, under the name of righteousness. 'Alms', first: that He begins with at the first verse, and so here it is first. Then, to 'prayer' next, at the fifth verse; and after that, to 'fasting', even as it is here too. Cornelius' works were these three: 'Gave alms'; 'prayed' duly; was found at his 'fast' by the Angel. This is all we find, more we find not specified; and these are enough, these would serve, if we would do them. These in him were, the same in us will be accepted.

And now, of God's acceptation. Accepting is but a quaint term borrowed from the Latin. It is no more than receiving or taking. First then, clear it is He will take them; but, where they be to take. But where they are not, take them He cannot. In vain shall we look for acceptation of that which is not. We are then to see there be some given, some for Him to take. Take us He cannot, if there be not Cornelius' hand to take us by; 'come up in remembrance' they cannot, if none were done to remember; for it is a 'remembrance of things past', and all ours are yet to come I fear, in 'fancy' rather than in 'remembrance'. Our 'alms', alas they are shrunk up pitifully; 'prayer', swallowed up with hearing lectures; and for the third, feast if you will continually, but 'fast' as little as may be; and of most I might say, not at all. The want of these, the bane of our age. He stretcheth out His hand, to receive 'alms'; He boweth down His ear, to receive 'prayer'; He beholdeth with His eyes, to take us 'fasting': there is none to give them, and so He cannot receive them. But, by this 'is accepted' here, we see how we might be 'accepted'.

It is beside the text; yet if ye ask, Here is fear, and here are works, where is faith all this while, 'without which it is impossible to please God', or 'to be accepted of Him'? Had he no faith? Yes, he would not have spent his goods, or chastened his body, without some faith; at least, 'call' God he could not, on Whom he 'believed' not.

Therefore he believed sure, the Gentiles' creed at least, that a God there is; that sought He will be; that He will not fail them that seek Him, but both regard and reward them.

Whitsun sermon 12, vol. 3, pp 336–9

A sermon prepared to be preached on Whitsunday 1622

The manifestation of the Spirit is given to every man to profit withal.

1 Corinthians 12.4–7

This sermon, which seems not to have been delivered, emphasizes the duty to accept and use the gifts of the Spirit as they are given proportionally. Typical of the period are the regard for order and hierarchy, and the reference to the four bodily humours.

I told you before, the callings were founded upon order, and to keep them so, have their limits or bounds. And they do all 'walk out of order', disorderly break the pales and over they go; that leaving their own, become, as St Peter's word is, 'Bishops of other men's dioceses'; do no good in their own, spend their time in finding fault with others. A thing not to be endured in anybody. Take the natural body for example, wherein the spirit, blood, choler, and other humours are to keep and contain themselves, to hold every one in his own proper vessel; as blood in the veins, choler in the gall. And if once they be out of them, the blood out of the vein makes an apostume; the choler out of the gall makes a jaundice all over the body. Believe it, this is an evil sickness under the sun, that the division of works is not kept more strictly. They are divided according to the callings; every work is not for every calling. For then what needs any dividing? But as the calling is, so are the works to be; every one to intend his own, wherein it is presumed his skill lies, and not to busy himself with others; for that is 'meddling'. And these are the three errors about 'operations'.

It will not be amiss if we look yet a little further into this word. For it is 'operation', which is more than 'work' is not every work; it is an in-wrought work. A work wrought by us so, as in us also. And both it may be. For 'working' and 'working together with' take not away one or the other. So then by ourselves, as by some other beside ourselves; and that is God, Who is said here to 'work all in all'.

'All in all'. If we take it at the uttermost extent it will reach, then we must be well aware to sever the defect or deformity of the work from the work itself; as well we may. Moving is the work, halting is the deformity. Moving, that comes from the soul, is wrought by it; halting, the deformity, not from the soul, whence the moving comes, but that ill caused by the crookedness of the leg. So is the evil of the work; the defect from us, the work from God, and that His.

But, of all good, all our well-wrought works, of them, we say not only, 'We can do none of them without Him'; but further, we say with the Prophet, 'Lord. Thou hast wrought all our works in us'. In them He doth not only co-operate with us from without, but even from within; as I may say, in-operate them in us; 'working in you'. Then, if there go another workman to them besides ourselves, we are not to take them wholly to ourselves. But if that other workman be God, we will allow Him for the principal workman at the least. That, upon the whole matter, if our ability be but of gift; if our calling be but a service; if our very work but 'operation', 'a thing wrought in us'; 'Babylon is fallen', pride falls to the ground: these three have laid it flat.

But besides this, there are three points more in 'operation'. I will touch them first. 'In us' they are said to be 'wrought', to show our works should not be screwed from us; wound out of us with some wrench from without, without which nothing would come from us by our will, if we could otherwise choose: 'works from without' these properly. But 'works from within'; hath the 'basis of motion' there, and thence; and so are natural and kindly works.

Next, from within; to show they are not taken-on works, done in hypocrisy; so the outside fair, what is within it skills not. But that there be 'truth in the inward parts', that there it be wrought, and that thence it come.

And last, if it be an 'operation' it hath an energy, that is, a workmanship, such as that the gift appears in it. For energy implies it is not done 'haphazard', but workman-like done. [. . .] And even the very word 'of division' comes to as much. Dividing implies skill to hit the joint right; for that is to divide. To cut at venture, quite beside the joint, it skills not where, through skin and bones and all; that is to chop and mangle, and not to divide. Division hath art ever. And this for God's division, the division of works. And so now you have all three.

We have set down the order. Will you now reflect upon it a little, and see the variation of the compass, and see how these divisions are all put out of order; and who be in, and who be out at everyone of them? First, whereas the gift and the calling are, and so are to be, relatives, neither without the other; there are men of no gifts to speak of that may seem to have come too late, or to have been away quite, at the first of the Spirit's dealing – no share they have of it; yet what do they? Fairly stride over the gifts, never care for them, and step into the calling over the gifts, and so over the Holy Ghost's head. Where they should begin with the gift, the first thing they begin with, is to get them a good place. Let the gift come after, if it will; or if it do not, it skills not greatly. They are well, they lie soaking in the broth in the mean time. This neglect of the gift, in effect, is a plain contempt of the Spirit, as if there were no great need of the Holy Ghost.

Thus it should be. As one speeds at the first division, so he should at the second. If no grace from the Spirit, no place with Christ. If some one, but a mean one, let his place be according. He with the two mites, not in the place of him with the 'five talents': or as one well expressed it, not little-learned Aurelius, Bishop of great Carthage, and great learned St Augustine, Bishop of little Hippo. This is a trespass sure against the first division, which respecteth not only the gifts in specie, but in measure too. Proportion the places to the proportion of the gifts; which proportion we know is both ways broken, whether a low gift have a high place, or a rich gift be let lie in a poor place; contrary to the mind of Christ, who would have the degree of the place as near as could be to the measure of the gift.

Whitsun sermon, 15 vol. 3, pp. 392–4

Before James I at Whitehall, Christmas Day 1616

Mercy and Truth are met together; Righteousness and Peace have kissed each other.

Psalm 85.10–11

A meditation on the necessity of the four virtues named in the Psalm ends with affirming the wholeness of the Christian faith and the danger of error through separation of revealed truths. Encratite: name given to several early Christian sects condemned as excessively ascetic.

And as it is a meeting so a cross meeting of four virtues that seem to be in a kind of opposition, as hath been noted. No matter for that. They will make the better refraction; the cool of one allay the heat, the moist of one temper the drought of the other. [. . .] So are the elements of which our body, so are the four winds of which our breath doth consist which gives us life. And these in the text have an analogy or correspondence with the elements, observed by the ancients. Truth as the 'earth, which is not moved at any time', 'peace as a water-stream', 'the quills whereof make glad the City of our God'. Mercy we breathe and live by, no less than we do by air; and Righteousness, she 'will come to judge the earth by fire' in that element.

You may happen to find one of these in Scripture stood much upon, and of the other three nothing said there, but all left out. Conceive of it as a figure, Synecdoche they call it. As ye have here man called earth; yet is he not earth alone, but all the other three elements as well. No more is Christianity any one but by Synecdoche, but in very deed a meeting of them all four.

It deceived the Gnostic, this place; 'This is eternal life, to know Thee'. Knowledge, saith he, is it, as if it were all; and so he bade care, for nothing else but to know, and knowing live as they list. The Encratite, he was as far gone the other way; he lived straightly, and his tenet was, 'So that ye hold a straight course of life, it skills not what ye hold in point of faith.' No meeting with these, single virtues all.

Yes, it skills. For both these were wrong, both go for heretics. Christianity is a meeting, and to this meeting there go pious beliefs as well as good works. Righteousness as well as Truth. Err not this error then, to single any out as it were in disgrace of the rest; say not, one will serve the turn, what should we do with the rest of the four? Take not a figure, and make of it a plain speech; seek not to be saved by Synecdoche. Each of these is a quarter of Christianity, you shall never while you live make it serve for the whole.

The truth is, sever them, and farewell all. Take any one from the rest, and it is as much as the whole is worth. For, as Bernard well observed, 'upon their separation they cease to be virtues'. For how loose a thing is mercy, if it be quite devoid of justice! We call it foolish pity. And how harsh a thing justice, if it be utterly without all temper of mercy! That is 'injustice: at the highest;' Mercy, take Truth away, what hold is there of it? Who will trust it? Truth, take Mercy from it, it is severity rather than verity. Then Righteousness without Peace, certainly wrong is much better – better than perpetual brabbling. And Peace without Righteousness, better a sword far. This, if you sunder them. But temper these together, and how blessed a mixture! Set a song of all four, and how heavenly melody!

Entertain them then all four: hope in Mercy; faith in Truth; fear of Righteousness; love of Peace. O how loving a knot! How by all means to be maintained! How great pity to part it!

A little of the time now, when this meeting would be. No time amiss, no day in the year but upon entreaty they will be got to meet. Yet if any one day have a prerogative more than another, of all the days in the year on this day most kindly; the day we hold holy to the memory of this meeting; the day of 'He is born', the occasion of it. In remembrance of the first meeting then, they are apt and willing to meet upon it again; forward ever to meet the day they first met of themselves. But Christ this day born, this day to meet of course. One special end that He was born was that at His birth this meeting might be. If to-day then they should not meet, that were in a sort to evacuate Christ's birth, if there should be 'Truth springing up' without 'they are met together'; so that if we procure it not, we had as good keep no feast at all.

What is then the proper work of this day, but still to renew this meeting on it? For Christ's birth we cannot entertain, but all these we must too, necessary attendants upon it every one. They be the virtues of His Nativity, these. At His birth Christ bethought himself of all the virtues which He would have to attend on Him then; and these He made choice of, then and for ever; to be the virtues of this feast . . .

The sooner and the better to procure this meeting, the Church meets us, as Melchizedek did Abraham, 'with bread and wine' but of a higher nature than his far; prepares ever this day a love-feast, whereat they may the rather meet. Where Truth from the earth may look up to Heaven and confess, and Righteousness from Heaven may look down to earth and pardon; where we may show Mercy in giving where need is; and offer Peace in forgiving where cause is; that so there may be, a 'meeting' of all hands.

And even so then let there be. So may our end be as the end of the first verse, in peace; and as the end of the second, in Heaven! So may all the blessings that came to mankind by this meeting, or by the birth of Christ the cause of it; meet in us and remain upon us, till as we now meet together at the birth; so we may then meet in a 'perfect man in the measure of the fullness of the age of Christ'; as meet now at the Lamb's yeaning, so meet then at the Lamb's marriage; 'be caught up in the clouds then to meet Him', and there to reign for ever with Him in His Kingdom of Glory!

Nativity sermon 11, vol. 1, pp. 192–5

Prepared to be preached on Easter Day 1624

Make you perfect in every good work to do His will, working in you that which is wellpleasing in His sight.

Hebrews 13.20–21

Near the end of his life, in another sermon which was not delivered, Andrewes was still insisting on the need for active good works as well as faith, being 'made perfect' by God in 'doing' what He wills. This is one of his most positive statements of the idea of being 'fellow-workers' with God.

What way doth God take to set us right? First, by our ministry and means. For it is a part of our profession under God, this same 'making perfect' to set the church in, and every member that is out of joint. You may read it in this very term, 'for the perfecting'. And that we do, by applying outwardly this Testament and the blood of it, two special splints as it were, to keep it straight. Out of the Testament, by 'the word of exhortation', as in the next verse he calls it, praying us, to suffer the splinting. For it may sometimes pinch them, and put them to some pain that are not well in joint, by pressing it and putting it home. But both by denouncing, one while the threats of the Old Testament, another while by laying forth the promises of the New, if by any means we may get them right again. This by the Testament, which is our outward means. The blood is another inward means. By it we are made fit and perfect, (choose you whether) and that so, as at no time of all our life we are so well in joint, or borne so near the state of perfectness, as when we come new from the drinking of that blood. And thus are we made fit.

Provided that 'to make perfect' do end, as here it doth, in 'making' and 'in work'; that all this fit-making do end in doing and in a work, that some work be done. For in doing it is to end, if it end aright; if it end as the Apostle here would have it. For this fitting is not to hear, learn, or know, but 'to do His will'. We have been long at 'Teach me Thy will', at that lesson. There is another in Psalm one hundred and forty-three, 'Teach me to do Thy will'; we must take out that also. 'Teach me Thy will', and 'Teach me to do Thy will', are two distinct lessons. We are all our life long about the first, and never come to the second, to 'in the doing'. It is required we should now come to the second, to 'in the doing'. We are not made fit, when we are so, to do never a whit the more; 'making perfect' is to end in 'doing', and, in 'a work'.

In work, and 'in every good work'. We must not slip the collar there, neither. For if we be able to stir our hand one way and not another, it is a sign it is not well set in. His that is well set, he can move it to and fro, up and down, forward and backward; every way, and to every work. There be that are all for some one work, that single some one piece of God's service, wholly addicted to that, but cannot skill of the rest. That is no good sign. To be for everyone, for all sorts of good works, for every part of God's worship alike, for no one more than another, that sure is the right. So choose your religion, so practise your worship of God. It is not safe to do otherwise, nor to serve God by Synecdoche; but 'in all things', to take all before us.

But in the doing of all or any, beside our part, 'in the doing' here is also 'working in you', a worker besides. For when God hath fitted us by the outward means, there is not all. He leaves not us to ourselves for the rest, but to that outward application of ours joins His 'working in you', an inward operation of His own inspiring, His grace, which is nothing but the breath of the Holy Ghost. Thereby enlightening our minds, inclining our wills, working on our affections, making us 'men of good will', that when we have done well, we may say with the Prophet, 'Lord, all our good works Thou hast wrought in us'. Our works they be, yet of

Thy working. And with the Apostle, 'we did them, yet not we, but the grace of God that was with us'. Both ways, it is true: what He works by us He works in us, and what He works in us He works by us. For 'working', 'working with', take not away one the other, but stand well together. This for the doing.

Now for the work. In every good work we do His will; the work yet, it seemeth, degrees there are. For here is mention of 'His will'; and besides it, of 'His good pleasure', and this latter sounds as if it did import more than a single will. One's good pleasure is more than his bare will. So in the chapter before he wisheth that 'we may serve and please'; that is, may so serve as that we may please. Acceptable service then is more than any, such as it is. There is no question but that, as of evil works some displease God more than other, so of good works there are some better pleasing, and that He takes a more special delight in.

And if you would know what they be, above at the sixteenth verse it is said that 'to do good and to distribute', that is, distributive doing good, it is more than an ordinary service; it is a sacrifice, every such work. It is of the highest kind of service, and that with that kind 'God is highly pleased'. So doth St Paul call the bounteous supplying of his wants from the Philippians, 'a sacrifice right acceptable and pleasing unto God' and 'a most delightful sweet savour'. And that you may still see He looks to the Resurrection, He saith, the Philippians had lain dead and dry a great while, as in winter trees do use. But when that work of bounty came from them, they did 'shoot forth, wax fresh, grow green again', as now at this season plants do. That so the very virtue of Christ's resurrection-time, the time of bringing things as it were from the dead again, with this of Christ. Which time is therefore the most pleasing time, the time of the greatest pleasure of all the times of the year. So, we know, how to do that is pleasing in His sight.

Yet even this pleasing and all else is to conclude, as here it doth, with 'through Jesus Christ our Lord'. He is here too. In, at the doing; in at the making them to please God 'that by what by Christ is done, by Christ may please when it is done'. In at the doing, 'by infusing or dropping in His grace active'; making us able and fit to do, and so to do them. In at the pleasing, 'by pouring on His good grace and favour passive', as it might be some drops of His blood, whereby it pleaseth being done. Gracing His work, as we use to say, in God's sight, that so He of His grace may crown it.

Resurrection sermon 18, vol. 3, pp. 97–9

10

Law and Government

With the idea of the 'godly prince', some of the churches of the Reformation asserted that the monarch could rightfully have power over Church affairs. Together with the belief in divine right, this caused Andrewes and other leading churchmen to give their views about the nature of sovereignty and the mutual duties of rulers and subjects.

Why rulers are appointed

We see the apostle goeth thus to work: God would have all men saved; that they might be saved, He would have them live in goodness and honesty; that they might so do, he would have them taught the knowledge of God; and that they might intend this, He would have them lead a peaceable and quiet life; peaceable in regard of outward invasions, and quiet in regard of inward tumults and troubles. Now if the natural father and natural mother could have performed this, they needed no other; but there comes one Nimrod, with a company of hounds at his tail (that metaphor it pleaseth the Holy Ghost to use) and he takes it upon him to be a hunter, that is a chaser of men, to disturb and trouble them; and later that God first allowed, and after instituted, that there should be:

Governors, to deliver us from unreasonable and evil men.

Government, both for resisting of outward foes, and for quieting of inward strifes; and to comfort and cherish good men, that love to live quietly, to come to knowledge of God, and of a religious demeanour of themselves.

The magistrate is the minister of God to take vengeance on them who do evil, but a cherisher and comforter of such as do well. The benefit received from his vigilance is well set forth, [by Daniel] under the representation of a great tree, and [by Isaiah] comparing him to a river in dry places, and the shadow of a great rock in a dry land. Our duty must be to give him all due submission and honour, for in his peace we shall have peace.

Duties of a king

And being thus qualified, and so meet for a kingdom, and set in his seat, his duties are:

First, to acknowledge his power to be from God.

To acknowledge himself to be there not by himself, but by God; 'by Me kings reign', saith God. And so their style runneth, 'Caesar, or chief governor, by the grace of God'; and that therefore their power is not 'arbitrary', or at their own pleasure, but 'delegate' and put upon him by God; and therefore he must say with the centurion, 'I myself also am under authority' they are under God, and therefore must so rule as God himself would rule; and how is that? Even as His word prescribeth and no otherwise.

The duty of the subject answerable is, to acknowledge him to be God's deputy – 'there went with him a band of men whose hearts God had touched' – and to reverence him accordingly.

Secondly, not to break into God's right.

The second duty of the prince is, Seeing God hath been so liberal to Caesar as to make him king and His deputy, he must not requite Him by breaking into that which is God's peculiar; for we see our Saviour maketh a division, 'some things to Caesar, some to God'; as namely the court of conscience; the Lord only keepeth His court there; and therefore the king must command nothing to any man against his conscience; yet those whose consciences are not well instructed, they must labour to rectify them, and if they be obstinate, and will not yield to religion, they must compel them; and if there be not 'a will within' there must be 'a necessity laid on them by others'; and therefore let papists come and hear, that they may be caught.

And generally, he must 'feed the people', that is, provide for them,

for their souls, that preachers be sent into all places;

for their bodies, he must

lay up corn against a dearth, and see there be plenty;

send ships abroad, for outward and foreign commodities;

and for inward right to all men at home, provide judges;

and to avoid wrongs from abroad, provide soldiers.

The people's duty answerable to these is,

That they break not into God's right, neither take the sword out of the king's hand; nor be seditious, or disobedient unto him 'fear God and the king, and be not seditious'.

In regard of their care over us, we must not 'give', but 'render to Caesar' that which 'is his due'; that is, because they keep our tillage safe, they must have tribute out of our lands, and because they keep the sea safe, they have 'custom', and 'subsidy', out of our goods; and in time of necessity, 'indiction' or tax.

Thirdly, to do justice.

The third duty of the king is, in cases of appeal to do justice himself; for that is it that must establish his throne, and without it 'great kingdoms', are nothing else but 'great robberies'. And in his justice he must look,

that the righteous may flourish, and that 'they which do well may have well';

to the wicked his looks must be terrible in judgement, that so he may drive away evil; for capital crimes, 'let not thine eye spare them'.

The people's duty herein is, in respect of his justice, to fear him, 'the wrath of a king is as messengers of death, but a wise man will pacify it'; 'the fear of a king is as the roaring of a lion; whoso provoketh him to anger sinneth against his own soul'.

Fourthly, to be humble and meek in ruling.

The fourth duty of the king is humility and meekness in ruling; to use his power meekly and mildly; not as Pilate, 'I have power to crucify thee, and I have power to loose thee'; but every magistrate should do well to say with Paul, 'I have no power to hurt, but to do good; to edification, and not to destruction'.

It is the difference that a heathen man maketh between a good king, and a tyrant; a tyrant saith, 'I may do it and I will do it'; the good king saith, 'I must do it, it is my duty, I pray you pardon me'.

To conclude, 'he who may do all things, may indeed do less than any man'. And if he will not be mild, but of an austere, cruel behaviour to his people, they may well fear him, but sure they will not love him, and then 'fear', may well breed 'flattery', but not 'true good will'.

The people's duty to such a mild king is,

(not to fear him, but) to be afraid of him, that is to say, in their love to him to be afraid lest any hurt should come unto him, as the people were afraid of David;

and another duty of the people is, to bear with the infirmities of this mild king, and to be as meek toward him in covering his uncomeliness if any be, unless it be some enormous sin, or that he be a troubler of Israel.

Thus much of the king's duty.

A Pattern of Catechistical Doctrine, pp. 175–6; 200–202

Before James I at Burleigh near Oakham, 5 August 1614

I have found David my servant; with My holy oil have I anointed him.

Psalm 89.20–23

Kings are 'found' by God alone, as part of the divine purpose. 'Invention' here means 'finding'.

If Kings be the invention of God, then are not their inventions of God – these I mean that have been broached of late – that find Kings, or found Kings upon any but God; that make Prophet, Priest or people King-finders, or King-founders, or ascribe this invention to any but to Him in the text. This for the Person, 'I have found'.

How 'found' the second? By hap? No, it is 'I have found'; in that word is the manner of it. Every tongue hath a proper word to sever things sought and so found, from things found without seeking. [. . .] David then was not, Kings are not, 'hit upon at adventure', or stumbled on by chance; they are not 'things of chance'. No, they are 'found'; first sought, and so found upon search. Will ye hear it 'in so many words'? Saith God of David, 'I have sought me out a man'.

Not that any is hid from Him, that He need seek him; it is but in our own phrase to express to our capacities, how God stood affected to the having of Kings. So set to have them that rather than not have them, He would do as we do, even take the pains to seek them out. Now, the endeavour to seek is from no velleity, no faint will; no, it is from a desire, that fain would find. And that desire is from no mean conceit; (if it come, so it is; if not, no great matter) but from some special good conceit we have of that we seek for; that we hold it worth the time we spend, worth the labour we bestow about it. All is but to show us the worth of this invention. For it is no mean thing, we may be sure, that God will seek. Seeking them, He shows He holds them, for such, as He would not be without them Himself; He would not have His people in any wise be without them. And that He would not have them thought as good lost as 'found', but esteemed for such by us, as if we had them not, we would, of His example, set ourselves to seek them seriously, and never leave till we have found them. This for the manner.

But then thirdly, seeking, why 'found' He David rather than any other? We find the reason of that in 'My servant', because He 'found' him His 'servant'. For a servant He sought, to whom He might commit the highest point of His service, the care of His people. And He 'found' him so zealous for His flock, to keep them from being a prey to strange beasts, as He thought him meet to be made of 'shepherd of sheep, shepherd of men'. He 'found' him so devout at His service that He set him in such a place, as if he were the servant of God, he might make ten thousand more beside himself.

These two words then, we may not slip over; the claim of the Covenant after lieth by them. And if the Covenant hath not been kept with any, it hath been for default of this, that He hath 'found' him; *him*, but not him His 'servant'.

Yea, if any King be 'found' by God before he do, or by use of nature can do Him any service, suppose in his cradle, yet even to such a one is not this word without fruit. It hath his use, this: it is the way not only in making them to be 'found', but in keeping them from being lost. For the same, that was the way to be 'found' at first, the very same is the way not to be lost ever after. And it concerns David, or any, as nearly, not to be lost again, as it doth at first to be 'found'.

Now if David look well to these two words, and lose them not, God will not lose him, he may be sure, but be at hand still ready to defend him. Unless David lose them, he cannot lose God; and unless he lose God, he cannot be lost. David ever lost them, before his enemies could do him any harm. All Balaam's cursing will do him no hurt; nothing but his wicked counsel, to unmake him His servant, and so to lose God, and so to be lost of God, and so to be lost, utterly lost. Lay up this then; the way to be 'protected by God' is to 'serve God'. And lay it up well, it is the only article of covenant on David's part; upon these two words depends all that follows, upon 'My servant'. If they be sure, all is sure, And this for 'finding'.

But I find here a 'proclamation of finding' besides. To find is one thing, to cry, *eureka*, 'I have found', another. One may find, and keep his own counsel: so men do for the most part. But God here proclaims His finding; tells all He hath 'found'. And none do so but such as are surprised with joy; as the party in the Canticles, 'I have found whom my soul sought', and I would the world knew it, I am not a little glad of it. Commonly, where there is care in seeking, as before, there is joy in finding. Joy then, and it is not joy alone, for one may 'keep his joy to himself', but 'joy with glory', this. For he not only joys in his invention, but glories in it, and even boasts of it, that doth 'proclaim finding'. The word which he useth, *eureka*, is made famous by Archimedes, who in a great passion between glorying and rejoicing first cried it, when he had found the secret of King Hiero's crown. But no less famous by St Andrew, who, upon the finding of Christ, came running to his brother

St Peter, with Archimedes' cry, 'We have found' Him 'the Messias', we have found Him. 'Messias' in Hebrew, is nothing else but anointed; and we shall see David 'anointed' straight. And sure, next to the joy of Christ, 'Christ the Lord' we may place the joy of 'anointed of the Lord', and take up our next *eureka* for him. God's word will well become us to use.

And to whom is this? To 'His Saints'; to them He tells it – look the last verse before. As if they had their part in this finding, so invites He them to the fellowship of the same joy. Tells them that such a one He had 'found'; and for them, and for their good He had 'found' him. They, to reap special benefit by it, by this finding; therefore, they to take special notice of it, they specially to rejoice with Him in it.

And what should I say but as this Psalm saith a little before, 'Blessed are the people that can skill of this joy', that can skill of their own good, what it is to have a King, a King found to their hand, but specially a king that is God's servant. Verily, if God's joy be our joy, it is to be with us as with God it was; this *eureka*, the *eureka* of joy. And truly, all this text, both that which is past, His care in seeking, and His joy in finding; and that which followeth, His honour in anointing, His mercy in making this covenant, His truth in keeping it, His rescuing them from, His revenging them upon their enemies; all is but to show us how much He doth, and if we will do as He doth, how much we are to do, even to set by, even to joy and pray with Him in, 'I have found David My servant'.

Gowrie sermon 4, vol. 4, pp. 80–83

Before James I at Greenwich, 5 August 1610

Touch not Mine anointed.

1 Chronicles 16.22

In this sermon his assertion of the divine right of kings is even firmer; he attacks the papal claim to have power to depose monarchs. Much is made of the contrast between ordinary anointing – unctus – and the holy anointing of christos.

His 'anointed' is more than His, for all His are not 'anointed'; for if all were 'anointed', there should be none left to 'touch' them, we might strike out this verse, the charge were in vain, there were none to receive it. If all be *uncti*, where should be 'the touchers'? We must then needs leave a difference between Christians and *christi*. For, holding all that are Christians, all God's people 'anointed' and 'holy' alike, it will follow, why should Moses then, or any, take upon him to be their superior? And so we fall into the old 'contradiction of Korah' which is all one with the new parity and confusion of the Anabaptists, or those that prick fast towards them.

But the very ceremony itself serveth to show, somewhat is added to them by which they be His, after a more peculiar manner than the rest, to whom that is not added. Oil itself designeth sovereignty. Pour together water, wine, vinegar, what liquor you will, oil will be uppermost. And that is added by their anointing. Besides then this general claim, 'Mine', here is His special signature 'anointed', whereby they are severed from the rest. His hand hath touched them with His anointing, that no other hand might 'touch' them. Things anointed of ourselves we forbear to touch; but specially if the anointing have the nature of a mark, that we wrong it not. And this hath so, these are so marked, that we might forbear them. And yet more specially, if we have a caveat not to do it, as here we have. 'Touch not them that I have anointed'.

This were all, if it were but 'anointed'; but there is yet a further matter than all this. For it is not *unctos* but My *christos*. We read it 'Mine anointed': in the Hebrew, Greek and Latin, it is more full. In Hebrew, 'My messiahs'; in Greek and Latin, 'My *christos*', that is, 'My christs', which is far more forcible. Somewhat we may be sure was in it, that all the old writers uniformly forbore to turn it *unctos*, which is enough for 'anointed', and all have agreed to turn it *christos*, 'christs', which is a great deal more. It seems they meant not to take a grain from this charge, but to give it his full weight. And it cannot but weigh much with all that shall weigh this one point well, that Princes are taken into the society of God's Name in the Psalm before, and here into the society of Christ's Name in this, and so made 'synonymous' both with God and with Christ; specially, since Himself it is That so styleth them, for He flatters not, we are sure. God Himself is a King, 'King of all the earth', and His Heir of all, as appeareth by His 'many crowns on His head'. Those whom God and Christ vouchsafe to take into the charge of any their Kingdoms, them they vouchsafe their own names of God and of Christ. They two the first Kings, to these other the after Kings, ruling under them and in their names.

A third gradual reason then there riseth here. All anointed are not 'christs', for all anointing is not chrism. Chrism is not every common, but an holy anointing, a sacred signature. 'With Mine holy oil have I anointed them'. 'Mine' to make them His, 'holy' to make them sacred. He might have taken this oil out of the apothecary's shop, or the merchant's warehouse. He did not, but from the Sanctuary itself, to show their calling is sacred, sacred as any, even the best of them all. From whence the Priests have theirs, thence and from no other place the King hath his – from the Sanctuary both. The anointing is one and the same. All to show that sacred is the office whereunto they designed, sacred the power wherewith they endued, sacred the persons whereto it applied. And for such were they held, all the primitive Church through. Their writ, 'the height of holiness', their word, 'divine command', their presence, 'the print of holiness': the usual style of the Councils, when they spake of them. And when they ceased to know themselves for His, That here saith 'Mine', and to hold of Him, then lost they their holiness; He that took from them the one, took to Himself the other. Now then will ye infer? Holy they be, their anointing hallowed; therefore 'Touch not Mine holy ones'. No more touch Moses than the holy Mount, which neither man nor beast might touch upon pain of death; no more touch David, than the holy Ark. It is not good touching of holy things. Uzzah so found it.

And yet still methinks we fall short, for it is not 'holy' neither, it is more than 'holy', it is *christos* in which word, there is more than in 'the communion of saints'. 'We cannot say of all Saints they be christs, of Kings we may.' Verily, every degree of holiness will not make a synonym with Christ. He was 'anointed' saith the Psalm, 'with a holy oil or chrism above His fellows'. To hold this name then of 'The Lord's christs', it is not every ordinary holiness will serve, but a special and extraordinary degree of it above the rest, which they are to participate, and so do from Christ, whose Name they bear, eminent above others that carry not that Name; as if they did in some kind of measure partake even 'such a chrism as wherewith Christ is anointed'. And the inference of this point, and the meaning of this style of 'gods' and 'christs' is, as if He would have us with a kind of analogy as careful in a manner to forbear touching them, as we would be to touch God, or the Son of God, Christ Himself. It is not then 'Mine', nor 'Mine anointed', nor 'My holy ones' only, but it is 'My christs', 'Mine', and that 'anointed', 'anointed with holy oil'; so 'anointed', and with oil so 'holy', as it raiseth them to the honour of the denomination of the holy of holies, Christ Himself. These four degrees, and from them these four several reasons, are in 'My christs'.

One thing more of 'My christs', for I should do you wrong certainly, if I should slip by it and not tell yon what this anointing is, and leave a point loose that needeth most of all to be touched. Upon misconceiving of this point some have fallen into a fancy, His 'anointed' may forfeit their tenure, and so cease to be His, and their anointing dry up, or be wiped off and so Kings be un-christed, cease to be 'the Lord's christs', and then who that will may touch them.

They that have been scribbling about Kings' matters of late, and touching them with their pens, have been foully mistaken in this point. Because anointing in Scripture doth otherwhile betoken some spiritual grace, they pitch upon that, upon that taking of the word; and then anointing, it must needs be some grace, some 'grace making acceptable', making them religious and good Catholics, or some 'grace freely given', making them able or apt for to govern. So that if he will not hear a Mass, no Catholic, no 'anointed'. If after he is 'anointed' he grow defective, to speak their own language, prove a tyrant, fall to favour heretics, his anointing may be wiped off, or scraped off; and then you may write a book *Concerning just deposition*, make a holy league, touch him, or blow him up as ye list. This hath cost Christendom dear, it is a dangerous sore, a 'Do not touch me', take heed of it, touch it not.

Gowrie sermon 3, vol. 4, pp. 54–6

Before James I at Whitehall, Christmas Day 1624

I will declare the decree.

Psalm 2.7

The regard which Andrewes had for the rule of law made him oppose those who deny the importance of the Law in Christianity. It may seem an unexpected defence when the Puritans were putting so much emphasis on the rules in both Testaments, but he recognized the danger of making the Gospel seem soft and undemanding.

'I will preach the law' saith Christ. And we like it well that He will preach. But He hath not chosen so good a text; 'law' were a fitter text for Moses to preach on. We had well hoped, Christ would have preached no law, all Gospel He. That He would have preached down the old Law, but not have preached up any new. We see it is otherwise. A law He hath to preach, and preach it He will. He saith it Himself, 'I will preach the law'.

So if we will be His auditors, He tells us plainly we must receive a law from His mouth. If we love not to hear of a law, we must go to some other Church; for in Christ's Church there a law is preached. Christ began, we must follow and say every one of us as He saith, 'I will declare the law'.

Nay, there is another point yet more strange. These very words here, 'Thou art My Son', are as good Gospel as any in the New Testament; yet are here, as we see, delivered by Him under the term of a law. And we may not change His word, we may not learn Christ how to use His terms. The words are plain, there is no avoiding them; a law He calls it, and a law it is.

First then, to take notice of both these. That Christ will preach a law, and that they that are not for the law, are not for Christ. It was their quarrel above, at the third verse, they would none of Christ for this very cause, that Christ comes preaching the law, and they would live lawless; they would endure, no yoke that were 'the sons of Belial'; 'Belial', that is no yoke; 'but what agreement hath Christ with Belial ?'

And then, that these words 'Thou art My Son' are a law, and so a law as by Christ preached. So as in the very Gospel itself, all is not Gospel, some law among it. The very Gospel hath her law. A law evangelical there is which Christ preached; and as He did, we to do the like. [. . .]

In the meantime it is not without danger to let such conceit take head as though Christian religion had no law-points in it, consisted only of pure narratives – believe them, and all is well; had but certain theses to be held, dogmatical points, matters of opinion. And true it is, such points there be, but they be not all. There is a law besides, and it hath precepts and they to be preached, learned, and as a law to be obeyed of all.

Look but into the grand commission by which we all preach, which Christ gave at His going out of the world; 'Go' saith He, 'preach the Gospel to all nations teaching' – what? 'to observe the things that I have commanded you'. Lo, here is commanding, and here is observing. So the Gospel consists not only of certain articles to be believed but of certain commandments also, and they to be observed. And what is that but 'I will preach the law'!

Now I know not how, but we are fallen clean from this term 'Law'; nay we are even now fallen out with it. Nothing but Gospel now. The name of Law, we look strangely at; we shun it in our common talk. To this it is come, while men seek to live as they list. Preach them Gospel as much as you will; but, hear ye, no 'I will preach the law', no law to be preached, to hold or keep them in. And we have gospelled it so long that the Christian Law is clean gone with us, we have lost it; if 'I will preach the law' get it us not again. But got it must be, for as Christ preacheth, so must we; and law it is that Christ preacheth.

I shall tell you what is come by the drowning of the term 'Law'. Religion is even come to be counted 'a matter of prayer'. No Law – no, no; but a matter of fair entreaty, gentle persuasion; neither judgements nor laws; but only 'good fatherly counsel', and nothing else. Evangelical counsels were a while laid aside; now there be none else. All are Evangelical counsels now. The reverend regard, the legal vigour and power, the penalties of it are not set by the rules – no reckoning made of them as of law-writs, none, but only as of physic bills; if you like them you may use them, if not, lay them by. And this comes of drowning the term 'Law'. And all, for lack of 'I will preach the law'.

I speak it to this end; to have the one term retained as well as the other, to have neither term abolished; but with equal regard, both kept on foot. They are not so well advised that seek to suppress either name. If the name once be lost, the thing itself will not long stay, but go after it, and be lost too.

They that take them to the one term only, are confuted once a month. For every month, every first day of every month, this verse faileth not but is read in our ears: And here a law it is. And so was the Christian religion called in the very best times of it, 'the Christian law'; and the Bishops, 'the Bishops of the Christian law'. And all the ancient Fathers liked the name well, and took it upon them.

To conclude. Gospel it how we will, if the Gospel hath not the legalities of it acknowledged, allowed, and preserved to it; if once it lose the force and vigour of a law, it is a sign it declines, it grows weak and unprofitable, and that is a sign it will not long last. We must go look our salvation by some other way than by 'Thou art My Son', if 'Thou art My Son' (I say not be not preached, but) be not so preached, as Christ preached it; and Christ preached it as a law. And so much for law.

Now of this law, three things are here said; first, law turns back upon 'I will preach'. And this privilege it hath, that it is a law which may, nay a law which 'is to be preached'. And that laws use not to be; not to be preached. To be read upon at times privately but to be preached, not any law but this. But this is, and it serves for a special difference to sever it from other laws, and make it a kind by itself. Even this, that it is to be preached.

To be preached; and that, even to Kings themselves that make laws; to judges themselves, that are presumed to be best seen in the law; yet they to learn, they to be learned in this law. 'Be instructed' is the word, '<you> who judge the world', in the tenth verse after.

And the reason is; for this is a law 'of which God speaks'. And so is none else. And that is a second difference. There is a law 'of which men speak', which men among themselves make for themselves, as by-laws are made. This is of a higher nature. This God Himself made, is a law of His own making.

Nativity sermon 17, vol. 1, pp. 287–90

Andrewes did not limit his sermons on State occasions to general issues. He frequently urged his hearers not to lapse into a passive acceptance of faith but to experience the working of God in their own lives as well as in public events.

Before James I at Whitehall, 5 November 1606

This is the day which the Lord hath made; we will rejoice and be glad in it.

Psalm 118.23–4

In his first Gunpowder Treason sermon he speaks of the special providence to be remembered on particular days.

'This merciful and gracious Lord', saith David, Psalm the one hundred and eleventh, verse the fourth, 'hath so done His marvelous works that they ought to be had', and kept 'in remembrance'; of keeping in remembrance, many ways there be: among the rest, this is one, of making days, set solemn days, to preserve memorable acts, that they be not eaten out by them, but ever revived with the turn of the year, and kept still fresh in continual memory. God Himself taught us this way. In remembrance of the great delivery from the destroying Angel, He Himself ordained the day of the Passover yearly to be kept. The Church by Him taught took the same way. In remembrance of the disappointing of Haman's bloody lots they likewise appointed the days of 'Purim', yearly to be kept. The like memorable mercy did He vouchsafe us; 'the Destroyer' passed over our dwellings this day, it is our Passover. Haman and his fellows had set the dice on us, and we by this time had been all in pieces: it is our 'Purim' day.

We have therefore well done and upon good warrant, to tread in the same steps, and by law to provide that this day should not die nor the memory thereof perish from ourselves or from our seed, but be consecrated to a perpetual memory, by a yearly acknowledgment to be made of it throughout all generations. In accomplishment of which order, we are all now here in the presence of God on this day that He first, by His act of doing, hath made; and we secondly, by our act of decreeing have made before Him, His holy Angels and men, to confess this His goodness, and ourselves eternally bound to Him for it. And being to confess it, with what words of Scripture can we better or fitter do it than those we have read out of this Psalm? Sure I could think of none fitter but even thus to say, 'that the Lord hath made'.

The treaty whereof may well be comprised in three points: The deed or 'doing'; 'The day'; and The duty. The deed, in these: 'This is the Lord's', &c. 'The day', these: 'This is the day', &c. The duty in the rest: 'Let us', &c. The other two reduced to 'the day', which is the centre of both. The 'doing' is the cause, the duty the consequent: from 'the day' groweth the duty.

To proceed orderly, we are to begin with 'the day'. For though in place it stand after the deed, yet to us it is first, our knowledge is *a posteriori*. The effect ever first, where it is the ground of the rest. Of 'the day' then first.

That such days there be, and how they come to be such. Then of the 'doing' that maketh them: wherein that of David's was, and that ours is no less, rather more.

Then of the duty, how to do it? by rejoicing and being glad; for so 'joy shall be full', these two make it full. How to take order, that we may long and often do it? by saying our , 'Hosanna', and 'Benedictus'; for those will make that 'our joy no man shall take from us'.

'This is the day': 'This'? Why, are not all days made by Him? Are there any days not made by Him? Why then say we, 'This is the day the Lord hath made'? Divide the days into natural and civil: the natural, some are clear and some are cloudy; the civil, some are lucky days, and some dismal. Be they fair or foul, glad or sad, as the poet calleth Him the great 'Father of days' hath made them both. How say we then of some one day above his fellow, 'This is the day', &c.?

No difference at all in the days, or in the months themselves; by nature they are all one. No more in November than another month; nor in the fifth, than in the fifteenth. All is in God's making. For as in the creation we see all are the works, and yet a plain difference between them for that, in the manner of making: some made with 'Let there be'

– 'let there be light', 'a firmament', 'dry land'; some with 'Let us make', with more ado, greater forecast and framing, as man, that masterpiece of His works, of whom therefore, in a different sense, it may be said, This is the creature which God hath made – suppose after a more excellent manner. In the very same manner it is with days: all are His making, all equal in that; but that letteth not but He may bestow a special 'let us make' upon some one day more than another, and so that day, by special prerogative, said to be indeed a 'day that God hath made'.

Now for God's making, it fareth with days as it doth with years. Some year, saith the Psalm, 'God crowneth with His goodness', maketh it more seasonable, healthful fruitful than other. And so for days: God leaveth a more sensible impression of His favour upon some one, more than many besides by doing upon it some marvellons work. And such a day on which God vouchsafeth some special 'was made' some great and public benefit, notable for the time present, memorable for the time to come, in that case, of that day, as if God had said 'Let us make this day', showed some workmanship done, some special cost on it, it may with an accent, with an emphasis be said, This verily is a day which God hath made, in comparison of which the rest are as if they were not, or at least were not of His making.

As for black and dismal days, days of sorrow and sad accidents, they are and may be counted, saith Job, for no days – nights rather, as having 'the shadow of death' upon them; or as if days, such as his were, which Satan had marred than 'which God had made'. And for common and ordinary days, wherein as there is no harm, so not any notable good, we rather say: they are gone forth from God, in the course of nature, as it were, with a 'let it be', than 'made' by Him specially with a 'let us make'. So evil days, no days or days marred, and common days, days, but no 'made' days; only those 'made' that crowned with some extraordinary great favour, and thereby get a dignity and exaltation above the rest; exempted out of the ordinary course of the calendar with a 'This is'. Such, in the Law, was the day of the Passover made by God, the head of the year. Such, in the Gospel, of Christ's resurrection 'made' by God 'the Lord's day'; and to it do all the Fathers apply this verse. And we had this day our Passover, and we had a resurrection or 'figure', as Isaac had. But I forbear to go further in the general. By this that hath been said, we may see there be days of which it may be safely said, 'This is the day', &c. and in what sense it may be said. Such there be then; that this of ours, one of them; that if it be we may so hold it, and do the duties that pertain to it.

Before James I at Whitehall, 5 November 1617

That we being delivered out of the hand of our enemies might serve Him without fear.

Luke 1.74–5

He returns to the virtue of keeping a special day, recalling the Armada as well as the Gunpowder Plot.

The keeping of this day, the meeting of this assembly, are both to acknowledge and profess that a 'deliverance' there hath been.

Nay, not one alone: two there have been, and two such as our eyes have seen, but our ears have not heard, neither could our fathers tell us of the like. Two such as no age ever saw, nor can be found in any story; that of 1588, this of 1605, both within the compass of seventeen years. One by strand, the other by land, as they say. From a fleet by sea, from 'a vault by land', as saith the Psalm, as well as from 'a vault at sea' – a summer and a winter deliverance; either of them, like this of Zachary's, able to bring *Benedictus* from a dumb man.

So 'delivered' we were. But a delivery is a thing at large though it be but from a mischance, from some heavy accident, it is a delivery. But if it be 'from our enemies' it is so much the more: as in that there is nothing but casualty, in these there is rancour and malice – they hate us; so this the greater danger by far.

And there is much in the enemies: of them some reach but at our states, lands or livelihoods; other some, nothing will satisfy but our lives. Every enemy is not mortal: where he is, the danger is deadly. Ours were such, sought to bring utter destruction on us; and not on us alone, but on ours; nor on us and ours only, but on the whole land in general.

Again, of such as be deadly, some are roaring enemies, the Psalm so calls them, such as threaten and proclaim their enmity like those in 1588. Others lurk like vipers that sting to death without any hissing at all, as were ours this day, which are the more dangerous a great deal.

This made it indeed to be more than 'delivered', ours. 'Delivered' which is properly 'set free', and freeing us but from servitude. This was more. Our death was sought, and we 'delivered' from death, and that a fearful death; unprepared, suddenly, in a moment, to be shattered to pieces. And yet it was 'delivered' too, in the proper sense; for upon the matter it was from both. The Prophet's division would have taken place in it. 'They that had been blown up, to death, they that had been left, to servitude', to a state more miserable than death itself. So in one 'deliverance' we had two. Both from that of Haman's lots, which were to death – one that was 'fire' in Greek – and from that of Babylon besides, which was thralldom and confusion. Thus were we 'delivered from our enemies'.

But 'from the hands of our enemies' is more than 'from our enemies' or the malice of an enemy be what will, if his 'hands' be weak or short, or we far enough from them, the matter is so much the less. But if we come within his reach, if he get us within his 'hands', then God have mercy on us.

Specially if there be in his 'hands' a knife thus engraven: *To cut the throats of the English heretics*, as in 1588 divers so engraven in Spanish were brought from the fleet and showed. Or if there be in his 'hands' a match ready to give fire to thirty barrels of powder, not so few. If the 'hands' be such, that is then a delivery not from our enemies only, but from their 'hands', or, as we say, from their very clutches. Ye will mark that through all the Psalms ever the part is still enforced; not from the lions, but from the lions' paws; from 'the horns of the unicorns', from the teeth of the dog; so here 'from the hands', from the bloody 'hands of our enemies'.

Further I say, it is more to be delivered 'from' their 'hands' than out of them. For if out, then in, first. They must first be in the 'hands', that are delivered out of them. But 'from them', that they may be from coming in them at all. The better deliverance of the twain. And that was ours, and that was Christ's: He is said to have 'loosed the sorrows of hell', 'not wherewith He was bound; but that He might be not at all bound with them', saith Augustine. So we, not by taking us out, but keeping us from, from their 'hands', 'from the hands of our enemies'.

Gunpowder sermon 9, vol. 4, pp. 366–7

II

Devotional

All Andrewes's early biographers agree about the intensity and devotion of his personal prayers. A few extracts from his published prayers, and some of his observations about prayer will confirm their judgement, and it is hoped may lead the reader to explore these sources more fully.

Points of Meditation before Prayer

Thou art careful about many things: but one thing is needful.

But we will give ourselves continually to prayer and to the ministry of the word.

Watch ye and pray always, that ye may be accounted worthy to escape the things that shall come to pass.

Love the Lord all thy life and call upon Him for thy salvation.

Humble thy soul greatly: for the vengeance of the ungodly is fire and worms.

A man can receive nothing except it be given.

If He prayed that was without sin, how much more ought a sinner to pray:

but God is a hearer, not of the voice, but of the heart.

More is done by groanings than by words:

to this end Christ groaned, for to give us an ensample of groaning.

It is not that God desireth us to be suppliant or loveth that we lie prostrate: the profit thereof is ours and it hath regard to our advantage.

Prayer goeth up, pity cometh down.

God's grace is richer than prayer: God always giveth more than He is asked.

God commandeth that thou ask, and teacheth what to ask, and promiseth what thou dost ask, and it displeaseth Him if thou ask not: and dost thou not ask notwithstanding?

Prayer is a summary of faith, an interpreter of hope.

It is not by paces but by prayers that God is come at.
Faith poureth out prayer and is grounded in prayer.
Therefore go on to labour fervently in prayers,
    always to pray and not to faint,
    in spirit and in truth.
Faith is the foundation and basis of prayer:
    the foundation of faith is the promise of God.
Lift up your hearts.
He that made us to live, the same taught us withal to pray.
The prayer of the humble pierceth the clouds.
Prayer is colloquy with God.

Preces Privatae, pp. 7–8

A Form of Morning Prayer

Commemoration

O Lord, the day is thine, and the night is thine:
    Thou hast prepared the light and the sun:
they continue this day according to thine ordinance,
    for all things serve Thee.
In the evening, in the morning and at noonday will I pray, and that
    instantly,
    and Thou, Lord, shalt hear the voice of my prayer:
unto Thee, O Lord, will I make my prayer ;
    early in the morning will I make my prayer unto Thee,
    and my voice shalt Thou hear.

Thanksgiving

Blessed art Thou, O Lord,
    which turnest the shadow of death into the morning,
    and dost renew the face of the earth:
    which hast delivered us from terror by night,
    from the pestilence that walketh in the darkness:
    which hath lightened our eyes that they sleep not in death:
    which hast made sleep to pass from our eyes
    and slumber from our eyelids.

Petition

Blot out, O Lord, as a thick cloud of night our transgressions
    and as a morning cloud our sins:
make us children of the day and of the light:
grant us to walk chastely and soberly as in the day.
Vouchsafe, O Lord, to keep us this day without sin.
Keep us from the arrow that flieth by day,
    and from the sickness that destroyeth in the noonday:
deliver us from the hand of the hunter and from the noisome
      pestilence:
    from the evil of this day keep us.
Today salvation and peace be to this house.
O let me hear thy lovingkindness,
    for in Thee is my trust:
show Thou me the way that I should walk in,
    for I raise my soul unto Thee.
Deliver me, O Lord, from mine enemies,
    for I flee unto Thee to hide me:
instruct me to do what things are pleasing in thy sight,
    for Thou art my God:
let thy loving Spirit lead me forth into the land of righteousness.
Regard thy servants and their works;
    and the grace and glorious majesty of the Lord our God be upon us:
prosper Thou the work of our hands upon us,
    O prosper Thou our handiwork.
Set a watch, O Lord, before my mouth
    and keep the door of my lips:
let my speech be with grace, sprinkled with salt,
    that I may know how I ought to answer every man:
let the converse of my mouth and the meditation of my heart
    be alway acceptable in thy sight,
    O Lord my redeemer.
The Lord preserve our going out and coming in
henceforth and for evermore. Amen.

Preces Privatae, pp. 38–9

Before penitential devotions

O Lord, my heart is ready:
  so the Psalmist;
But, Lord, I fear that mine is not:
  I desire indeed, and I grieve if it be not
  Would God it were ready! woe is me that it is not!
O Lord, I dispose me and prepare:
  help Thou my disposition and supply my preparation.
I will set my sins before me,
  so that they be not before Thee.

Preces Privatae, p. 129

For the Quick and the Dead

Thou that art Lord at once of the living and of the dead;
whose are we whom the present world yet holdeth in the flesh;
whose are they withal whom, unclothed of the body,
  the world to come hath even now received:
give to the living mercy and grace,
  to the dead rest and light perpetual:
give to the Church truth and peace,
  to us sinners penitence and pardon.

Preces Privatae, p. 273

Concerning prayers of petition

The second branch of Invocation is Precation, which is the desiring of some thing that is good. There is no one thing more common in the Psalms than this; as, 'Give me understanding'. So 'Establish the thing that thou hast wrought in us, &c'. As the first prayer is to give what we want; so the second is, establish and confirm it in us when we have it. The third is that of the Apostles, to our Saviour, 'Lord, increase our faith in us'. We must not keep at a stand in grace, but desire an increment, that we may grow in grace, as the Apostle counselleth us.

Concerning that part of prayer, petition of the good we want, it is true, our desires are not always granted; for as Christ answered the sons of Zebedee, 'Ye ask ye know not what', so it may be said to us, we often desire rather that which is agreeable to our own humours than to God's will; as Chrysostom reports of a Thief, who purposing to continue in his sin, he prayed that he might not be taken, and was taken so much the sooner, because he so prayed.

Therefore the rule we must follow, and whereon we must ground our prayer is that promise, Whatsoever we ask according to his will, He will grant us: such are the graces of His spirit, and whatsoever is necessary to salvation, as the Word, Sacraments, public Worship, &c. These are that 'one thing necessary' which the Psalmist so earnestly begged, 'One thing have I desired of the Lord'. He desired many things, but one thing especially, to dwell in the house of God all the days of his life, to continue in the Church of God all his life, where he might glorify God, and work out his own salvation. Whatsoever is absolutely necessary to these ends, we may safely ask, and be sure God will grant, and therefore our Saviour tells us, that God grants His Spirit to those that ask Him, this is one thing which He will not deny us.

Now with these, or after these, we may pray for temporal things, that is, we pray first, for a competency, not for superfluity. The Patriarch Jacob prayed only for food and raiment, and Agur the son of Jakeh prays, give me neither poverty nor riches, but a sufficiency only, whereupon St Augustine saith, it is no unbeseeming prayer, because he asks only so much and no more. We must desire them with condition, if God see it expedient, submitting to His will; as Christ, 'If it be possible, and if it be Thy will': so did David praying for restitution to his kingdom. 'If I have found favour in the eyes of the Lord, He will bring me again, &c. if not, here I am, let Him do what seemeth good to Him'. He resigns all to God's will, and there is no more compendious way to obtain what we need, than to resign all to God's pleasure, whatsoever means we use, or however we struggle, nothing will avail without this. [. . .]

It seems strange that everyone that asks shall have, and that whatsoever he asks he shall have, seeing it is certain that many ask and have not.

We must remember that of St Augustine, that our duty is to pray however; for as he saith, Doth not God command thee to pray, and is he displeased if thou prayest not, and will he not deny thee what thou prayest for, and yet dost thou not pray?

We must know that the cause why we receive not, is not in his promise, but in our asking. 'Ye ask and receive not, because ye ask amiss', saith St James. For it is not a demonstrative sign of God's favour to us, to have all we desire granted; for we see that the Israelites desired flesh, and flesh God sent them, but it was with displeasure: for while the meat was yet in their mouths, the wrath of God came upon them, and slew the mightiest of them, and smote down the chosen men of Israel. And upon the people's violent desire to have a king, God gave them one, but in displeasure. Nay it is so far from a favour, that God sometimes grants the Devils (whom he favours not) their requests; as in the case of Job and the Swine.

And as this is not an absolute sign of favour, so God's denying of our requests, is not always a sign of his displeasure. This we may see in St Paul, who obtained not that he desired concerning the prick in the flesh. One reason St Isidore and St Aug<ustine> give; God oftimes hears not many as they desire, that He may hear them to their good. Another reason is given by St Aug<ustine> God denies not, but only defers to grant, that we might by his deferring them, ask and esteem of them more highly. Desire increaseth by delay, and things soon given are of light esteem: and therefore he adds, God keeps for thee, that He will not give thee quickly, that thou mayest learn with more affection to desire great things.

A Pattern of Catechistical Doctrine, pp. 13–14

Concerning thanksgiving

Thanksgiving is the last point of prayer.

God's glory is the chiefest end; and therefore, whether we receive before we ask, or when we ask, it is reason we consider, 'what shall I return unto the Lord?'

The heathen could say, 'a thankful mind is all which a kind and good heart aimeth at'. And it is the condition of the obligation wherein God hath bound Himself by His promise to hear us, 'thou shalt glorify Me'; so that if thou dost not glorify Him by thanksgiving, thou breakest the covenant, and art an usurper.

Thanksgiving standeth in four things.

Confession, that we have received it from heaven, and not from ourselves; as Austin saith, 'as he that confesseth that he hath that which he hath not, is rash; so he that denieth that he hath what he enjoyeth, is unthankful: therefore we must use what we have as things given us, not as things springing from ourselves, as things that are another's and not our own'.

Contentation, when we rest in the gifts of God, and are satisfied with that which we have, 'the lines are fallen unto me in pleasant places, yea I have a goodly heritage'.

Annunciation, to tell it to others what God hath done for us; 'come and hear, all ye that fear God, and I will declare what He hath done for my soul';

– in the congregation, 'I will praise the Lord with my whole heart, in the assembly of the upright, and in the congregation';

– yea to all nations, 'I will praise Thee, O Lord, among the people, I will sing unto Thee among the nations';

– yea to all posterity, 'they shall come, and shall declare His righteousness unto a people that shall be born, that He hath done this'; not to keep close the graces of God.

Exhortation to others to do the like; 'O come, let us sing unto the Lord, let us make a joyful noise to the Rock of our salvation'; and if there were no men, we should call upon the creatures to praise God.

Thanks is never truly given to God, but there is a better thing received; as Bernard saith, 'upon the ascending of thanks followeth a descending of grace'; and grace fails when our thanks fail.

The excellency of thanksgiving

The excellency of thanksgiving is well to be considered.

Chrysostom asking the question, Why David was called a man after God's own heart? answereth, Because David saw thanksgiving most of all pleased God, and therefore used it most of all; he esteemed prayer as an excellent thing, and appointed certain hours thereunto, yet he preferred the praising of God above all, and therefore used it seven times a day.

And for this cause, the Christian church, and innumerable angels, yea all the creatures in heaven, earth, and sea, sang praises, saying 'praise, and honour, and glory, and power be unto Him that sitteth upon the throne and unto the Lamb'.

Hence David counted his tongue exercised in the praises of God the best member which he had; therefore in the church of God every man should speak of His praise.

And this was the reason why the fathers ended with a doxology, 'Now to Jesus Christ with the Father and Holy Ghost, be given all honour, praise, glory'; etc 'for evermore'.

A Pattern of Catechistical Doctrine, pp. 103–5

An Act of Charity

Thyself O my God, Thyself for thine own sake, above all things else I love. Thyself I desire. Thyself as my last end I long for. Thyself for thine own sake, not aught else whatsoever, always and in all things I seek, with all my heart and marrow, with groaning and weeping, with unbroken toil and grief. What wilt Thou render me therefore for my last end? If Thou render me not Thyself, Thou renderest nought: if Thou give me not Thyself, Thou givest nought: if I find not Thyself, I find nought. To no purpose Thou rewardest me, but dost wring me sore. For, or ever I sought Thee, I hoped to find Thee at the last and to keep Thee: and with this honeyed hope in all my toils was I sweetly comforted. But now, if Thou have denied me Thyself, what else soever Thou give me, frustrate of so high a hope, and that not for a little space but for ever, shall I not always languish with love, mourn with languishing, grieve with mourning, bewail with grief, and weep for that always I shall abide empty and void? Shall I not sorrow inconsolably, complain unceasingly, be wrung unendingly? This is not thy property, O best, most gracious, most loving God: in no sort is it congruous, no wise it sorteth. Make me therefore, O best my God, in the life present always to love Thyself for Thyself before all things, to seek Thee in all things, and at the last in the life to come to find and to keep Thee for ever.

A Pattern of Catechistical Doctrine, p. 192

Before James I at Whitehall, 5 November 1615

His mercies are over all His works.

Psalm 145.9

The closing prayer of a 'Gunpowder Plot' sermon moves from specific and strongly physical thanksgiving to develop into an act of total praise. It is a suitable final example of how Andrewes continually moves between the immediate situation and the eternal verities of faith.

But we are not able to praise Thee, O Lord, or to extol Thy Name, for one of a thousand. Nay, not for one of the many millions of great mercies which Thou hast showed upon us and upon our children. How often hast Thou rid us from plague, freed us from famine, saved us from the sword, from our enemies compassing us round, from the fleet that came to make us no more a people!

Even before this day we now hold, before it and since it have not Thy compassions withdrawn themselves from us. But this day, this day above all days, have they showed it 'over all', and not over but upon us.

Wherefore the powers Thou hast distributed in our souls, the breath of life Thou hast breathed into our nostrils, the tongues Thou hast put into our mouths, behold all these shall break forth, and confess, and bless and thank, and praise, and magnify, and exalt Thee and Thy mercy for ever. Yea every mouth shall acknowledge Thee, every tongue be a trumpet of Thy praise, every eye look up, every knee bow, every stature stoop to Thee, and all hearts shall fear Thee. And all that within us, even our bowels, these our bowels that but for Thee had flown we know not whither; even our bones, those bones that but for it had been shivered bone from bone, one from another, all shall say, 'Who is like unto Thee, O Lord', in mercy? 'Who is like unto Thee, glorious in holiness, fearful in praise, doing wonders', wonders of mercy upon us this day, upon us all, to be held by us and our posterity in an everlasting remembrance?

Glory be to Thee, O Lord, glory be to Thee; glory be to Thee, and glory be to Thy mercy, the 'over all', the most glorious of all Thy great and high perfections. Glory be to Thee, and glory be to it – to it in Thee, and to Thee for it; and that by all Thy works, in all places and at all times. And of all Thy works, and above them all by us here; by the hearts and lungs of us all. In this place, this day for this day, for the mercy of this day; for the mercy of it above all mercies, and for the work of this day above all the works of it. And not this day only, but all the days of our life, even as long as Thy mercy endureth, and that 'endureth for ever' – for ever in this world, for ever in the world to come; 'through' the cistern and conduit of all Thy mercies, Jesus Christ.

Gunpowder Treason sermon 7, vol. 4, pp. 339–40

Glossary

aquisite	acquired
apostume	abscess
apprize	value, appreciate
avow	maintain
Austin	St Augustine of Hippo
bedesman	petitioner
behoof	benefit
behooved	was desirable
bewray	betray
brabbling	disputing aggressively
cardiack	of the heart
conceited	excited; also in modern sense of 'vain'
confounded	overthrown
cratch	manger
Cyclopian	gigantic, monstrous
elench	a refuting argument
embassage	diplomatic or political mission
enthwiting	reproach
Elias	the prophet Elijah
Esay	the prophet Isaiah
evict	prove
gomer	Old Testament measure, usually 'homer'
indiction	levy of tax
Jeremy	the prophet Jeremiah
laver	baptism
let	prevent, hinder; but also used in modern sense of 'permit'

linsey-woolsey	cloth of mixed wool and flax; thus, unsatisfactory mixture
Maran	Marano, Spanish Jew converted to Christianity, usually under constraint
mured	enclosed
Nilus	the river Nile
Osee	the prophet Hosea
otherwhile	sometimes, occasionally
phrenzy	frenzy
port-sale	auction sale
quiddity	quibble; also real nature, essence
quills	streams
remembrancer	reminder
seisin	taking possession
semblant	appearance, outward aspect
semblably	seemingly
skill (verb)	matter
skippers	seafarers
specie	particular quality
spleen	dislike, objection
stitch	spite
strand	shore
terrene	earthly
treaty	discussion
trow	believe or pledge
velleity	wishing
wot	know
wrench	forced or false interpretation
writhe	twist
yeaning	giving birth
Zachary	the prophet Zechariah

Further reading

A. M. Allchin, 'Lancelot Andrewes', in G. Rowell (ed.), *The English Religious Tradition and the Genius of Anglicanism*, Wantage: Ikon, 1992

B. Blackstone, 'Some Notes on Lancelot Andrewes', *Theology*, March 1950

J. W. Blench, *Preaching in England in the Late Fifteenth and Sixteenth Centuries*, Oxford: Blackwell, 1964

R. W. Church, 'Lancelot Andrewes', in A. Barry (ed.), *Masters in English Theology*, 1877, pp. 61–112

H. Davies, *Worship and Theology in England*, vol. 2, Princeton NJ: University of Princeton Press, 1973

M. Dorman, *Lancelot Andrewes: A Perennial Preacher of the Post-Reformation English Church*, Tucson: Fenestra Books, 2004

T. S. Eliot, *For Lancelot Andrewes: Essays on Style and Order*, London: Faber, 1928

W. H. Frere, *Bishop Lancelot Andrewes as a Representative of Anglican Principles*, London: SPCK, 1897

A. F. Herr, *The Elizabethan Sermon*, Philadelphia: Pennsylvania University Press, 1969, p. 140

F. Higham, *Lancelot Andrewes*, London: SCM Press, 1952

D. M. Loades, *Politics and the Nation: 1450–1660*, London: Collins, 1974

N. Lossky, *Lancelot Andrewes the Preacher: The Origins of the Mystical Theology of the Church of England*, Oxford: Clarendon Press, 1991

D. Macleane, *Lancelot Andrewes and the Reaction*, London: George Allen, 1910

H. R. MacAdoo, *The Spirit of Anglicanism*, London: A. and C. Black, 1965

P. McCullough (ed.), *Lancelot Andrewes: Selected Sermons and Lectures*, Oxford: OUP, 2005

W. F. Mitchell, *English Pulpit Oratory from Andrewes to Tillotson*, London: SPCK, 1932

J. B. Mozley, 'Sermons of Lancelot Andrewes', *British Critic* 31:61, January 1842

W. H. Ness, 'Lancelot Andrewes and the English Church', *Theology*, September 1926

J. F. H. New, *Anglican and Puritan*, London: A. and C. Black, 1964

R. L. Ottley, *Lancelot Andrewes* (1894), 2nd edn, London: Methuen, 1905

M. F. Reidy, *Bishop Lancelot Andrewes: Jacobean Court Preacher*, Chicago: Loyola University Press, 1955

G. M. Story (ed.), *Lancelot Andrewes: Sermons*, Oxford: Clarendon Press, 1967

H. Veale (ed.), *The Devotions of Bishop Andrewes*, Cambridge: Deighton Bell, 1899

P. A. Welsby, 'Great Preachers: Lancelot Andrewes', *Theology*, August 1952

P. A. Welsby, 'Bishop Lancelot Andrewes and the Public Worship of the Church', *Theology*, April 1955

P. A. Welsby, 'Lancelot Andrewes and the Nature of Kingship', *Church Quarterly Review*, April–December 1955

P. A. Welsby, *Lancelot Andrewes, 1555–1626*, London: SPCK, 1958

A. Whyte, *Lancelot Andrewes and his Private Devotions*, Edinburgh: Oliphant Anderson and Ferrier, 1896; new edn, Kessinger, 2006